C-1543 CAREER EXAMINATION SERIES

This is your
PASSBOOK for...

Senior Research Analyst

Test Preparation Study Guide
Questions & Answers

COPYRIGHT NOTICE

This book is SOLELY intended for, is sold ONLY to, and its use is RESTRICTED to individual, bona fide applicants or candidates who qualify by virtue of having seriously filed applications for appropriate license, certificate, professional and/or promotional advancement, higher school matriculation, scholarship, or other legitimate requirements of education and/or governmental authorities.

This book is NOT intended for use, class instruction, tutoring, training, duplication, copying, reprinting, excerption, or adaptation, etc., by:

1) Other publishers
2) Proprietors and/or Instructors of "Coaching" and/or Preparatory Courses
3) Personnel and/or Training Divisions of commercial, industrial, and governmental organizations
4) Schools, colleges, or universities and/or their departments and staffs, including teachers and other personnel
5) Testing Agencies or Bureaus
6) Study groups which seek by the purchase of a single volume to copy and/or duplicate and/or adapt this material for use by the group as a whole without having purchased individual volumes for each of the members of the group
7) Et al.

Such persons would be in violation of appropriate Federal and State statutes.

PROVISION OF LICENSING AGREEMENTS – Recognized educational, commercial, industrial, and governmental institutions and organizations, and others legitimately engaged in educational pursuits, including training, testing, and measurement activities, may address request for a licensing agreement to the copyright owners, who will determine whether, and under what conditions, including fees and charges, the materials in this book may be used them. In other words, a licensing facility exists for the legitimate use of the material in this book on other than an individual basis. However, it is asseverated and affirmed here that the material in this book CANNOT be used without the receipt of the express permission of such a licensing agreement from the Publishers. Inquiries re licensing should be addressed to the company, attention rights and permissions department.

All rights reserved, including the right of reproduction in whole or in part, in any form or by any means, electronic or mechanical, including photocopying, recording, or by any information storage and retrieval system, without permission in writing from the Publisher.

Copyright © 2025 by
National Learning Corporation

212 Michael Drive, Syosset, NY 11791
(516) 921-8888 • www.passbooks.com
E-mail: info@passbooks.com

PASSBOOK® SERIES

THE *PASSBOOK® SERIES* has been created to prepare applicants and candidates for the ultimate academic battlefield – the examination room.

At some time in our lives, each and every one of us may be required to take an examination – for validation, matriculation, admission, qualification, registration, certification, or licensure.

Based on the assumption that every applicant or candidate has met the basic formal educational standards, has taken the required number of courses, and read the necessary texts, the *PASSBOOK® SERIES* furnishes the one special preparation which may assure passing with confidence, instead of failing with insecurity. Examination questions – together with answers – are furnished as the basic vehicle for study so that the mysteries of the examination and its compounding difficulties may be eliminated or diminished by a sure method.

This book is meant to help you pass your examination provided that you qualify and are serious in your objective.

The entire field is reviewed through the huge store of content information which is succinctly presented through a provocative and challenging approach – the question-and-answer method.

A climate of success is established by furnishing the correct answers at the end of each test.

You soon learn to recognize types of questions, forms of questions, and patterns of questioning. You may even begin to anticipate expected outcomes.

You perceive that many questions are repeated or adapted so that you can gain acute insights, which may enable you to score many sure points.

You learn how to confront new questions, or types of questions, and to attack them confidently and work out the correct answers.

You note objectives and emphases, and recognize pitfalls and dangers, so that you may make positive educational adjustments.

Moreover, you are kept fully informed in relation to new concepts, methods, practices, and directions in the field.

You discover that you are actually taking the examination all the time: you are preparing for the examination by "taking" an examination, not by reading extraneous and/or supererogatory textbooks.

In short, this PASSBOOK®, used directedly, should be an important factor in helping you to pass your test.

SENIOR RESEARCH ANALYST

DUTIES
An employee in this class performs difficult research and statistics work in the interpretation and analysis of assembled data to make projections concerning the future needs of the agency and/or the community. The incumbent is responsible for developing and conducting research studies and surveys designed to collect data that will aid in the evaluation of agency programs, community projects and their related programs. The incumbent may supervise a small staff of technical and clerical personnel. Performs related work as required.

SCOPE OF THE EXAMINATION
The written test will be designed to test for knowledge, skills, and/or abilities in such areas as:
1. Descriptive and inferential statistics;
2. Research and experimental design;
3. Understanding and interpreting tabular material;
4. Preparing written material; and
5. Supervision.

HOW TO TAKE A TEST

I. YOU MUST PASS AN EXAMINATION

A. *WHAT EVERY CANDIDATE SHOULD KNOW*

Examination applicants often ask us for help in preparing for the written test. What can I study in advance? What kinds of questions will be asked? How will the test be given? How will the papers be graded?

As an applicant for a civil service examination, you may be wondering about some of these things. Our purpose here is to suggest effective methods of advance study and to describe civil service examinations.

Your chances for success on this examination can be increased if you know how to prepare. Those "pre-examination jitters" can be reduced if you know what to expect. You can even experience an adventure in good citizenship if you know why civil service exams are given.

B. *WHY ARE CIVIL SERVICE EXAMINATIONS GIVEN?*

Civil service examinations are important to you in two ways. As a citizen, you want public jobs filled by employees who know how to do their work. As a job seeker, you want a fair chance to compete for that job on an equal footing with other candidates. The best-known means of accomplishing this two-fold goal is the competitive examination.

Exams are widely publicized throughout the nation. They may be administered for jobs in federal, state, city, municipal, town or village governments or agencies.

Any citizen may apply, with some limitations, such as the age or residence of applicants. Your experience and education may be reviewed to see whether you meet the requirements for the particular examination. When these requirements exist, they are reasonable and applied consistently to all applicants. Thus, a competitive examination may cause you some uneasiness now, but it is your privilege and safeguard.

C. *HOW ARE CIVIL SERVICE EXAMS DEVELOPED?*

Examinations are carefully written by trained technicians who are specialists in the field known as "psychological measurement," in consultation with recognized authorities in the field of work that the test will cover. These experts recommend the subject matter areas or skills to be tested; only those knowledges or skills important to your success on the job are included. The most reliable books and source materials available are used as references. Together, the experts and technicians judge the difficulty level of the questions.

Test technicians know how to phrase questions so that the problem is clearly stated. Their ethics do not permit "trick" or "catch" questions. Questions may have been tried out on sample groups, or subjected to statistical analysis, to determine their usefulness.

Written tests are often used in combination with performance tests, ratings of training and experience, and oral interviews. All of these measures combine to form the best-known means of finding the right person for the right job.

II. HOW TO PASS THE WRITTEN TEST

A. NATURE OF THE EXAMINATION

To prepare intelligently for civil service examinations, you should know how they differ from school examinations you have taken. In school you were assigned certain definite pages to read or subjects to cover. The examination questions were quite detailed and usually emphasized memory. Civil service exams, on the other hand, try to discover your present ability to perform the duties of a position, plus your potentiality to learn these duties. In other words, a civil service exam attempts to predict how successful you will be. Questions cover such a broad area that they cannot be as minute and detailed as school exam questions.

In the public service similar kinds of work, or positions, are grouped together in one "class." This process is known as *position-classification*. All the positions in a class are paid according to the salary range for that class. One class title covers all of these positions, and they are all tested by the same examination.

B. FOUR BASIC STEPS

1) Study the announcement

How, then, can you know what subjects to study? Our best answer is: "Learn as much as possible about the class of positions for which you've applied." The exam will test the knowledge, skills and abilities needed to do the work.

Your most valuable source of information about the position you want is the official exam announcement. This announcement lists the training and experience qualifications. Check these standards and apply only if you come reasonably close to meeting them.

The brief description of the position in the examination announcement offers some clues to the subjects which will be tested. Think about the job itself. Review the duties in your mind. Can you perform them, or are there some in which you are rusty? Fill in the blank spots in your preparation.

Many jurisdictions preview the written test in the exam announcement by including a section called "Knowledge and Abilities Required," "Scope of the Examination," or some similar heading. Here you will find out specifically what fields will be tested.

2) Review your own background

Once you learn in general what the position is all about, and what you need to know to do the work, ask yourself which subjects you already know fairly well and which need improvement. You may wonder whether to concentrate on improving your strong areas or on building some background in your fields of weakness. When the announcement has specified "some knowledge" or "considerable knowledge," or has used adjectives like "beginning principles of…" or "advanced … methods," you can get a clue as to the number and difficulty of questions to be asked in any given field. More questions, and hence broader coverage, would be included for those subjects which are more important in the work. Now weigh your strengths and weaknesses against the job requirements and prepare accordingly.

3) Determine the level of the position

Another way to tell how intensively you should prepare is to understand the level of the job for which you are applying. Is it the entering level? In other words, is this the position in which beginners in a field of work are hired? Or is it an intermediate or advanced level? Sometimes this is indicated by such words as "Junior" or "Senior" in the class title. Other jurisdictions use Roman numerals to designate the level – Clerk I, Clerk II, for example. The word "Supervisor" sometimes appears in the title. If the level is not indicated by the title, check the description of duties. Will you be working under very close supervision, or will you have responsibility for independent decisions in this work?

4) Choose appropriate study materials

Now that you know the subjects to be examined and the relative amount of each subject to be covered, you can choose suitable study materials. For beginning level jobs, or even advanced ones, if you have a pronounced weakness in some aspect of your training, read a modern, standard textbook in that field. Be sure it is up to date and has general coverage. Such books are normally available at your library, and the librarian will be glad to help you locate one. For entry-level positions, questions of appropriate difficulty are chosen – neither highly advanced questions, nor those too simple. Such questions require careful thought but not advanced training.

If the position for which you are applying is technical or advanced, you will read more advanced, specialized material. If you are already familiar with the basic principles of your field, elementary textbooks would waste your time. Concentrate on advanced textbooks and technical periodicals. Think through the concepts and review difficult problems in your field.

These are all general sources. You can get more ideas on your own initiative, following these leads. For example, training manuals and publications of the government agency which employs workers in your field can be useful, particularly for technical and professional positions. A letter or visit to the government department involved may result in more specific study suggestions, and certainly will provide you with a more definite idea of the exact nature of the position you are seeking.

III. KINDS OF TESTS

Tests are used for purposes other than measuring knowledge and ability to perform specified duties. For some positions, it is equally important to test ability to make adjustments to new situations or to profit from training. In others, basic mental abilities not dependent on information are essential. Questions which test these things may not appear as pertinent to the duties of the position as those which test for knowledge and information. Yet they are often highly important parts of a fair examination. For very general questions, it is almost impossible to help you direct your study efforts. What we can do is to point out some of the more common of these general abilities needed in public service positions and describe some typical questions.

1) General information

Broad, general information has been found useful for predicting job success in some kinds of work. This is tested in a variety of ways, from vocabulary lists to questions about current events. Basic background in some field of work, such as sociology or economics, may be sampled in a group of questions. Often these are principles which have become familiar to most persons through exposure rather than through formal training. It is difficult to advise you how to study for these questions; being alert to the world around you is our best suggestion.

2) Verbal ability

An example of an ability needed in many positions is verbal or language ability. Verbal ability is, in brief, the ability to use and understand words. Vocabulary and grammar tests are typical measures of this ability. Reading comprehension or paragraph interpretation questions are common in many kinds of civil service tests. You are given a paragraph of written material and asked to find its central meaning.

3) Numerical ability

Number skills can be tested by the familiar arithmetic problem, by checking paired lists of numbers to see which are alike and which are different, or by interpreting charts and graphs. In the latter test, a graph may be printed in the test booklet which you are asked to use as the basis for answering questions.

4) Observation

A popular test for law-enforcement positions is the observation test. A picture is shown to you for several minutes, then taken away. Questions about the picture test your ability to observe both details and larger elements.

5) Following directions

In many positions in the public service, the employee must be able to carry out written instructions dependably and accurately. You may be given a chart with several columns, each column listing a variety of information. The questions require you to carry out directions involving the information given in the chart.

6) Skills and aptitudes

Performance tests effectively measure some manual skills and aptitudes. When the skill is one in which you are trained, such as typing or shorthand, you can practice. These tests are often very much like those given in business school or high school courses. For many of the other skills and aptitudes, however, no short-time preparation can be made. Skills and abilities natural to you or that you have developed throughout your lifetime are being tested.

Many of the general questions just described provide all the data needed to answer the questions and ask you to use your reasoning ability to find the answers. Your best preparation for these tests, as well as for tests of facts and ideas, is to be at your physical and mental best. You, no doubt, have your own methods of getting into an exam-taking mood and keeping "in shape." The next section lists some ideas on this subject.

IV. KINDS OF QUESTIONS

Only rarely is the "essay" question, which you answer in narrative form, used in civil service tests. Civil service tests are usually of the short-answer type. Full instructions for answering these questions will be given to you at the examination. But in case this is your first experience with short-answer questions and separate answer sheets, here is what you need to know:

1) Multiple-choice Questions

Most popular of the short-answer questions is the "multiple choice" or "best answer" question. It can be used, for example, to test for factual knowledge, ability to solve problems or judgment in meeting situations found at work.

A multiple-choice question is normally one of three types—
- It can begin with an incomplete statement followed by several possible endings. You are to find the one ending which *best* completes the statement, although some of the others may not be entirely wrong.
- It can also be a complete statement in the form of a question which is answered by choosing one of the statements listed.

- It can be in the form of a problem – again you select the best answer.

Here is an example of a multiple-choice question with a discussion which should give you some clues as to the method for choosing the right answer:

When an employee has a complaint about his assignment, the action which will *best* help him overcome his difficulty is to
    A. discuss his difficulty with his coworkers
    B. take the problem to the head of the organization
    C. take the problem to the person who gave him the assignment
    D. say nothing to anyone about his complaint

In answering this question, you should study each of the choices to find which is best. Consider choice "A" – Certainly an employee may discuss his complaint with fellow employees, but no change or improvement can result, and the complaint remains unresolved. Choice "B" is a poor choice since the head of the organization probably does not know what assignment you have been given, and taking your problem to him is known as "going over the head" of the supervisor. The supervisor, or person who made the assignment, is the person who can clarify it or correct any injustice. Choice "C" is, therefore, correct. To say nothing, as in choice "D," is unwise. Supervisors have and interest in knowing the problems employees are facing, and the employee is seeking a solution to his problem.

2) True/False Questions

The "true/false" or "right/wrong" form of question is sometimes used. Here a complete statement is given. Your job is to decide whether the statement is right or wrong.

SAMPLE: A roaming cell-phone call to a nearby city costs less than a non-roaming call to a distant city.

This statement is wrong, or false, since roaming calls are more expensive.

This is not a complete list of all possible question forms, although most of the others are variations of these common types. You will always get complete directions for answering questions. Be sure you understand *how* to mark your answers – ask questions until you do.

V. RECORDING YOUR ANSWERS

Computer terminals are used more and more today for many different kinds of exams.
For an examination with very few applicants, you may be told to record your answers in the test booklet itself. Separate answer sheets are much more common. If this separate answer sheet is to be scored by machine – and this is often the case – it is highly important that you mark your answers correctly in order to get credit.

An electronic scoring machine is often used in civil service offices because of the speed with which papers can be scored. Machine-scored answer sheets must be marked with a pencil, which will be given to you. This pencil has a high graphite content which responds to the electronic scoring machine. As a matter of fact, stray dots may register as answers, so do not let your pencil rest on the answer sheet while you are pondering the correct answer. Also, if your pencil lead breaks or is otherwise defective, ask for another.

Since the answer sheet will be dropped in a slot in the scoring machine, be careful not to bend the corners or get the paper crumpled.

The answer sheet normally has five vertical columns of numbers, with 30 numbers to a column. These numbers correspond to the question numbers in your test booklet. After each number, going across the page are four or five pairs of dotted lines. These short dotted lines have small letters or numbers above them. The first two pairs may also have a "T" or "F" above the letters. This indicates that the first two pairs only are to be used if the questions are of the true-false type. If the questions are multiple choice, disregard the "T" and "F" and pay attention only to the small letters or numbers.

Answer your questions in the manner of the sample that follows:

32. The largest city in the United States is
    A. Washington, D.C.
    B. New York City
    C. Chicago
    D. Detroit
    E. San Francisco

1) Choose the answer you think is best. (New York City is the largest, so "B" is correct.)
2) Find the row of dotted lines numbered the same as the question you are answering. (Find row number 32)
3) Find the pair of dotted lines corresponding to the answer. (Find the pair of lines under the mark "B.")
4) Make a solid black mark between the dotted lines.

VI. BEFORE THE TEST

Common sense will help you find procedures to follow to get ready for an examination. Too many of us, however, overlook these sensible measures. Indeed, nervousness and fatigue have been found to be the most serious reasons why applicants fail to do their best on civil service tests. Here is a list of reminders:

- Begin your preparation early – Don't wait until the last minute to go scurrying around for books and materials or to find out what the position is all about.
- Prepare continuously – An hour a night for a week is better than an all-night cram session. This has been definitely established. What is more, a night a week for a month will return better dividends than crowding your study into a shorter period of time.
- Locate the place of the exam – You have been sent a notice telling you when and where to report for the examination. If the location is in a different town or otherwise unfamiliar to you, it would be well to inquire the best route and learn something about the building.
- Relax the night before the test – Allow your mind to rest. Do not study at all that night. Plan some mild recreation or diversion; then go to bed early and get a good night's sleep.
- Get up early enough to make a leisurely trip to the place for the test – This way unforeseen events, traffic snarls, unfamiliar buildings, etc. will not upset you.
- Dress comfortably – A written test is not a fashion show. You will be known by number and not by name, so wear something comfortable.

- Leave excess paraphernalia at home – Shopping bags and odd bundles will get in your way. You need bring only the items mentioned in the official notice you received; usually everything you need is provided. Do not bring reference books to the exam. They will only confuse those last minutes and be taken away from you when in the test room.
- Arrive somewhat ahead of time – If because of transportation schedules you must get there very early, bring a newspaper or magazine to take your mind off yourself while waiting.
- Locate the examination room – When you have found the proper room, you will be directed to the seat or part of the room where you will sit. Sometimes you are given a sheet of instructions to read while you are waiting. Do not fill out any forms until you are told to do so; just read them and be prepared.
- Relax and prepare to listen to the instructions
- If you have any physical problem that may keep you from doing your best, be sure to tell the test administrator. If you are sick or in poor health, you really cannot do your best on the exam. You can come back and take the test some other time.

VII. AT THE TEST

The day of the test is here and you have the test booklet in your hand. The temptation to get going is very strong. Caution! There is more to success than knowing the right answers. You must know how to identify your papers and understand variations in the type of short-answer question used in this particular examination. Follow these suggestions for maximum results from your efforts:

1) Cooperate with the monitor

The test administrator has a duty to create a situation in which you can be as much at ease as possible. He will give instructions, tell you when to begin, check to see that you are marking your answer sheet correctly, and so on. He is not there to guard you, although he will see that your competitors do not take unfair advantage. He wants to help you do your best.

2) Listen to all instructions

Don't jump the gun! Wait until you understand all directions. In most civil service tests you get more time than you need to answer the questions. So don't be in a hurry. Read each word of instructions until you clearly understand the meaning. Study the examples, listen to all announcements and follow directions. Ask questions if you do not understand what to do.

3) Identify your papers

Civil service exams are usually identified by number only. You will be assigned a number; you must not put your name on your test papers. Be sure to copy your number correctly. Since more than one exam may be given, copy your exact examination title.

4) Plan your time

Unless you are told that a test is a "speed" or "rate of work" test, speed itself is usually not important. Time enough to answer all the questions will be provided, but this does not mean that you have all day. An overall time limit has been set. Divide the total time (in minutes) by the number of questions to determine the approximate time you have for each question.

5) Do not linger over difficult questions

If you come across a difficult question, mark it with a paper clip (useful to have along) and come back to it when you have been through the booklet. One caution if you do this – be sure to skip a number on your answer sheet as well. Check often to be sure that you have not lost your place and that you are marking in the row numbered the same as the question you are answering.

6) Read the questions

Be sure you know what the question asks! Many capable people are unsuccessful because they failed to *read* the questions correctly.

7) Answer all questions

Unless you have been instructed that a penalty will be deducted for incorrect answers, it is better to guess than to omit a question.

8) Speed tests

It is often better NOT to guess on speed tests. It has been found that on timed tests people are tempted to spend the last few seconds before time is called in marking answers at random – without even reading them – in the hope of picking up a few extra points. To discourage this practice, the instructions may warn you that your score will be "corrected" for guessing. That is, a penalty will be applied. The incorrect answers will be deducted from the correct ones, or some other penalty formula will be used.

9) Review your answers

If you finish before time is called, go back to the questions you guessed or omitted to give them further thought. Review other answers if you have time.

10) Return your test materials

If you are ready to leave before others have finished or time is called, take ALL your materials to the monitor and leave quietly. Never take any test material with you. The monitor can discover whose papers are not complete, and taking a test booklet may be grounds for disqualification.

VIII. EXAMINATION TECHNIQUES

1) Read the general instructions carefully. These are usually printed on the first page of the exam booklet. As a rule, these instructions refer to the timing of the examination; the fact that you should not start work until the signal and must stop work at a signal, etc. If there are any *special* instructions, such as a choice of questions to be answered, make sure that you note this instruction carefully.

2) When you are ready to start work on the examination, that is as soon as the signal has been given, read the instructions to each question booklet, underline any key words or phrases, such as *least, best, outline, describe* and the like. In this way you will tend to answer as requested rather than discover on reviewing your paper that you *listed without describing*, that you selected the *worst* choice rather than the *best* choice, etc.

3) If the examination is of the objective or multiple-choice type – that is, each question will also give a series of possible answers: A, B, C or D, and you are called upon to select the best answer and write the letter next to that answer on your answer paper – it is advisable to start answering each question in turn. There may be anywhere from 50 to 100 such questions in the three or four hours allotted and you can see how much time would be taken if you read through all the questions before beginning to answer any. Furthermore, if you come across a question or group of questions which you know would be difficult to answer, it would undoubtedly affect your handling of all the other questions.

4) If the examination is of the essay type and contains but a few questions, it is a moot point as to whether you should read all the questions before starting to answer any one. Of course, if you are given a choice – say five out of seven and the like – then it is essential to read all the questions so you can eliminate the two that are most difficult. If, however, you are asked to answer all the questions, there may be danger in trying to answer the easiest one first because you may find that you will spend too much time on it. The best technique is to answer the first question, then proceed to the second, etc.

5) Time your answers. Before the exam begins, write down the time it started, then add the time allowed for the examination and write down the time it must be completed, then divide the time available somewhat as follows:
    - If 3-1/2 hours are allowed, that would be 210 minutes. If you have 80 objective-type questions, that would be an average of 2-1/2 minutes per question. Allow yourself no more than 2 minutes per question, or a total of 160 minutes, which will permit about 50 minutes to review.
    - If for the time allotment of 210 minutes there are 7 essay questions to answer, that would average about 30 minutes a question. Give yourself only 25 minutes per question so that you have about 35 minutes to review.

6) The most important instruction is to *read each question* and make sure you know what is wanted. The second most important instruction is to *time yourself properly* so that you answer every question. The third most important instruction is to *answer every question*. Guess if you have to but include something for each question. Remember that you will receive no credit for a blank and will probably receive some credit if you write something in answer to an essay question. If you guess a letter – say "B" for a multiple-choice question – you may have guessed right. If you leave a blank as an answer to a multiple-choice question, the examiners may respect your feelings but it will not add a point to your score. Some exams may penalize you for wrong answers, so in such cases *only*, you may not want to guess unless you have some basis for your answer.

7) Suggestions
    a. Objective-type questions
        1. Examine the question booklet for proper sequence of pages and questions
        2. Read all instructions carefully
        3. Skip any question which seems too difficult; return to it after all other questions have been answered
        4. Apportion your time properly; do not spend too much time on any single question or group of questions

5. Note and underline key words – *all, most, fewest, least, best, worst, same, opposite,* etc.
6. Pay particular attention to negatives
7. Note unusual option, e.g., unduly long, short, complex, different or similar in content to the body of the question
8. Observe the use of "hedging" words – *probably, may, most likely,* etc.
9. Make sure that your answer is put next to the same number as the question
10. Do not second-guess unless you have good reason to believe the second answer is definitely more correct
11. Cross out original answer if you decide another answer is more accurate; do not erase until you are ready to hand your paper in
12. Answer all questions; guess unless instructed otherwise
13. Leave time for review

b. Essay questions
1. Read each question carefully
2. Determine exactly what is wanted. Underline key words or phrases.
3. Decide on outline or paragraph answer
4. Include many different points and elements unless asked to develop any one or two points or elements
5. Show impartiality by giving pros and cons unless directed to select one side only
6. Make and write down any assumptions you find necessary to answer the questions
7. Watch your English, grammar, punctuation and choice of words
8. Time your answers; don't crowd material

8) Answering the essay question

Most essay questions can be answered by framing the specific response around several key words or ideas. Here are a few such key words or ideas:

M's: manpower, materials, methods, money, management
P's: purpose, program, policy, plan, procedure, practice, problems, pitfalls, personnel, public relations

a. Six basic steps in handling problems:
1. Preliminary plan and background development
2. Collect information, data and facts
3. Analyze and interpret information, data and facts
4. Analyze and develop solutions as well as make recommendations
5. Prepare report and sell recommendations
6. Install recommendations and follow up effectiveness

b. Pitfalls to avoid
1. *Taking things for granted* – A statement of the situation does not necessarily imply that each of the elements is necessarily true; for example, a complaint may be invalid and biased so that all that can be taken for granted is that a complaint has been registered

2. *Considering only one side of a situation* – Wherever possible, indicate several alternatives and then point out the reasons you selected the best one
3. *Failing to indicate follow up* – Whenever your answer indicates action on your part, make certain that you will take proper follow-up action to see how successful your recommendations, procedures or actions turn out to be
4. *Taking too long in answering any single question* – Remember to time your answers properly

IX. AFTER THE TEST

Scoring procedures differ in detail among civil service jurisdictions although the general principles are the same. Whether the papers are hand-scored or graded by machine we have described, they are nearly always graded by number. That is, the person who marks the paper knows only the number – never the name – of the applicant. Not until all the papers have been graded will they be matched with names. If other tests, such as training and experience or oral interview ratings have been given, scores will be combined. Different parts of the examination usually have different weights. For example, the written test might count 60 percent of the final grade, and a rating of training and experience 40 percent. In many jurisdictions, veterans will have a certain number of points added to their grades.

After the final grade has been determined, the names are placed in grade order and an eligible list is established. There are various methods for resolving ties between those who get the same final grade – probably the most common is to place first the name of the person whose application was received first. Job offers are made from the eligible list in the order the names appear on it. You will be notified of your grade and your rank as soon as all these computations have been made. This will be done as rapidly as possible.

People who are found to meet the requirements in the announcement are called "eligibles." Their names are put on a list of eligible candidates. An eligible's chances of getting a job depend on how high he stands on this list and how fast agencies are filling jobs from the list.

When a job is to be filled from a list of eligibles, the agency asks for the names of people on the list of eligibles for that job. When the civil service commission receives this request, it sends to the agency the names of the three people highest on this list. Or, if the job to be filled has specialized requirements, the office sends the agency the names of the top three persons who meet these requirements from the general list.

The appointing officer makes a choice from among the three people whose names were sent to him. If the selected person accepts the appointment, the names of the others are put back on the list to be considered for future openings.

That is the rule in hiring from all kinds of eligible lists, whether they are for typist, carpenter, chemist, or something else. For every vacancy, the appointing officer has his choice of any one of the top three eligibles on the list. This explains why the person whose name is on top of the list sometimes does not get an appointment when some of the persons lower on the list do. If the appointing officer chooses the second or third eligible, the No. 1 eligible does not get a job at once, but stays on the list until he is appointed or the list is terminated.

X. HOW TO PASS THE INTERVIEW TEST

The examination for which you applied requires an oral interview test. You have already taken the written test and you are now being called for the interview test – the final part of the formal examination.

You may think that it is not possible to prepare for an interview test and that there are no procedures to follow during an interview. Our purpose is to point out some things you can do in advance that will help you and some good rules to follow and pitfalls to avoid while you are being interviewed.

What is an interview supposed to test?

The written examination is designed to test the technical knowledge and competence of the candidate; the oral is designed to evaluate intangible qualities, not readily measured otherwise, and to establish a list showing the relative fitness of each candidate – as measured against his competitors – for the position sought. Scoring is not on the basis of "right" and "wrong," but on a sliding scale of values ranging from "not passable" to "outstanding." As a matter of fact, it is possible to achieve a relatively low score without a single "incorrect" answer because of evident weakness in the qualities being measured.

Occasionally, an examination may consist entirely of an oral test – either an individual or a group oral. In such cases, information is sought concerning the technical knowledges and abilities of the candidate, since there has been no written examination for this purpose. More commonly, however, an oral test is used to supplement a written examination.

Who conducts interviews?

The composition of oral boards varies among different jurisdictions. In nearly all, a representative of the personnel department serves as chairman. One of the members of the board may be a representative of the department in which the candidate would work. In some cases, "outside experts" are used, and, frequently, a businessman or some other representative of the general public is asked to serve. Labor and management or other special groups may be represented. The aim is to secure the services of experts in the appropriate field.

However the board is composed, it is a good idea (and not at all improper or unethical) to ascertain in advance of the interview who the members are and what groups they represent. When you are introduced to them, you will have some idea of their backgrounds and interests, and at least you will not stutter and stammer over their names.

What should be done before the interview?

While knowledge about the board members is useful and takes some of the surprise element out of the interview, there is other preparation which is more substantive. It *is* possible to prepare for an oral interview – in several ways:

1) Keep a copy of your application and review it carefully before the interview

This may be the only document before the oral board, and the starting point of the interview. Know what education and experience you have listed there, and the sequence and dates of all of it. Sometimes the board will ask you to review the highlights of your experience for them; you should not have to hem and haw doing it.

2) Study the class specification and the examination announcement

Usually, the oral board has one or both of these to guide them. The qualities, characteristics or knowledges required by the position sought are stated in these documents. They offer valuable clues as to the nature of the oral interview. For example, if the job involves supervisory responsibilities, the announcement will usually indicate that knowledge of modern supervisory methods and the qualifications of the candidate as a supervisor will be tested. If so, you can expect such questions, frequently in the form of a hypothetical situation which you are expected to solve. NEVER go into an oral without knowledge of the duties and responsibilities of the job you seek.

3) Think through each qualification required

Try to visualize the kind of questions you would ask if you were a board member. How well could you answer them? Try especially to appraise your own knowledge and background in each area, *measured against the job sought*, and identify any areas in which you are weak. Be critical and realistic – do not flatter yourself.

4) Do some general reading in areas in which you feel you may be weak

For example, if the job involves supervision and your past experience has NOT, some general reading in supervisory methods and practices, particularly in the field of human relations, might be useful. Do NOT study agency procedures or detailed manuals. The oral board will be testing your understanding and capacity, not your memory.

5) Get a good night's sleep and watch your general health and mental attitude

You will want a clear head at the interview. Take care of a cold or any other minor ailment, and of course, no hangovers.

What should be done on the day of the interview?

Now comes the day of the interview itself. Give yourself plenty of time to get there. Plan to arrive somewhat ahead of the scheduled time, particularly if your appointment is in the fore part of the day. If a previous candidate fails to appear, the board might be ready for you a bit early. By early afternoon an oral board is almost invariably behind schedule if there are many candidates, and you may have to wait. Take along a book or magazine to read, or your application to review, but leave any extraneous material in the waiting room when you go in for your interview. In any event, relax and compose yourself.

The matter of dress is important. The board is forming impressions about you – from your experience, your manners, your attitude, and your appearance. Give your personal appearance careful attention. Dress your best, but not your flashiest. Choose conservative, appropriate clothing, and be sure it is immaculate. This is a business interview, and your appearance should indicate that you regard it as such. Besides, being well groomed and properly dressed will help boost your confidence.

Sooner or later, someone will call your name and escort you into the interview room. *This is it.* From here on you are on your own. It is too late for any more preparation. But remember, you asked for this opportunity to prove your fitness, and you are here because your request was granted.

What happens when you go in?

The usual sequence of events will be as follows: The clerk (who is often the board stenographer) will introduce you to the chairman of the oral board, who will introduce you to the other members of the board. Acknowledge the introductions before you sit down. Do not be surprised if you find a microphone facing you or a stenotypist sitting by. Oral interviews are usually recorded in the event of an appeal or other review.

Usually the chairman of the board will open the interview by reviewing the highlights of your education and work experience from your application – primarily for the benefit of the other members of the board, as well as to get the material into the record. Do not interrupt or comment unless there is an error or significant misinterpretation; if that is the case, do not hesitate. But do not quibble about insignificant matters. Also, he will usually ask you some question about your education, experience or your present job – partly to get you to start talking and to establish the interviewing "rapport." He may start the actual questioning, or turn it over to one of the other members. Frequently, each member undertakes the questioning on a particular area, one in which he is perhaps most competent, so you can expect each member to participate in the examination. Because time is limited, you may also expect some rather abrupt switches in the direction the questioning takes, so do not be upset by it. Normally, a board member will not pursue a single line of questioning unless he discovers a particular strength or weakness.

After each member has participated, the chairman will usually ask whether any member has any further questions, then will ask you if you have anything you wish to add. Unless you are expecting this question, it may floor you. Worse, it may start you off on an extended, extemporaneous speech. The board is not usually seeking more information. The question is principally to offer you a last opportunity to present further qualifications or to indicate that you have nothing to add. So, if you feel that a significant qualification or characteristic has been overlooked, it is proper to point it out in a sentence or so. Do not compliment the board on the thoroughness of their examination – they have been sketchy, and you know it. If you wish, merely say, "No thank you, I have nothing further to add." This is a point where you can "talk yourself out" of a good impression or fail to present an important bit of information. Remember, *you close the interview yourself*.

The chairman will then say, "That is all, Mr. _____, thank you." Do not be startled; the interview is over, and quicker than you think. Thank him, gather your belongings and take your leave. Save your sigh of relief for the other side of the door.

How to put your best foot forward
Throughout this entire process, you may feel that the board individually and collectively is trying to pierce your defenses, seek out your hidden weaknesses and embarrass and confuse you. Actually, this is not true. They are obliged to make an appraisal of your qualifications for the job you are seeking, and they want to see you in your best light. Remember, they must interview all candidates and a non-cooperative candidate may become a failure in spite of their best efforts to bring out his qualifications. Here are 15 suggestions that will help you:

1) Be natural – Keep your attitude confident, not cocky
If you are not confident that you can do the job, do not expect the board to be. Do not apologize for your weaknesses, try to bring out your strong points. The board is interested in a positive, not negative, presentation. Cockiness will antagonize any board member and make him wonder if you are covering up a weakness by a false show of strength.

2) Get comfortable, but don't lounge or sprawl
Sit erectly but not stiffly. A careless posture may lead the board to conclude that you are careless in other things, or at least that you are not impressed by the importance of the occasion. Either conclusion is natural, even if incorrect. Do not fuss with your clothing, a pencil or an ashtray. Your hands may occasionally be useful to emphasize a point; do not let them become a point of distraction.

3) Do not wisecrack or make small talk
This is a serious situation, and your attitude should show that you consider it as such. Further, the time of the board is limited – they do not want to waste it, and neither should you.

4) Do not exaggerate your experience or abilities

In the first place, from information in the application or other interviews and sources, the board may know more about you than you think. Secondly, you probably will not get away with it. An experienced board is rather adept at spotting such a situation, so do not take the chance.

5) If you know a board member, do not make a point of it, yet do not hide it

Certainly you are not fooling him, and probably not the other members of the board. Do not try to take advantage of your acquaintanceship – it will probably do you little good.

6) Do not dominate the interview

Let the board do that. They will give you the clues – do not assume that you have to do all the talking. Realize that the board has a number of questions to ask you, and do not try to take up all the interview time by showing off your extensive knowledge of the answer to the first one.

7) Be attentive

You only have 20 minutes or so, and you should keep your attention at its sharpest throughout. When a member is addressing a problem or question to you, give him your undivided attention. Address your reply principally to him, but do not exclude the other board members.

8) Do not interrupt

A board member may be stating a problem for you to analyze. He will ask you a question when the time comes. Let him state the problem, and wait for the question.

9) Make sure you understand the question

Do not try to answer until you are sure what the question is. If it is not clear, restate it in your own words or ask the board member to clarify it for you. However, do not haggle about minor elements.

10) Reply promptly but not hastily

A common entry on oral board rating sheets is "candidate responded readily," or "candidate hesitated in replies." Respond as promptly and quickly as you can, but do not jump to a hasty, ill-considered answer.

11) Do not be peremptory in your answers

A brief answer is proper – but do not fire your answer back. That is a losing game from your point of view. The board member can probably ask questions much faster than you can answer them.

12) Do not try to create the answer you think the board member wants

He is interested in what kind of mind you have and how it works – not in playing games. Furthermore, he can usually spot this practice and will actually grade you down on it.

13) Do not switch sides in your reply merely to agree with a board member

Frequently, a member will take a contrary position merely to draw you out and to see if you are willing and able to defend your point of view. Do not start a debate, yet do not surrender a good position. If a position is worth taking, it is worth defending.

14) Do not be afraid to admit an error in judgment if you are shown to be wrong

The board knows that you are forced to reply without any opportunity for careful consideration. Your answer may be demonstrably wrong. If so, admit it and get on with the interview.

15) Do not dwell at length on your present job

The opening question may relate to your present assignment. Answer the question but do not go into an extended discussion. You are being examined for a *new* job, not your present one. As a matter of fact, try to phrase ALL your answers in terms of the job for which you are being examined.

Basis of Rating

Probably you will forget most of these "do's" and "don'ts" when you walk into the oral interview room. Even remembering them all will not ensure you a passing grade. Perhaps you did not have the qualifications in the first place. But remembering them will help you to put your best foot forward, without treading on the toes of the board members.

Rumor and popular opinion to the contrary notwithstanding, an oral board wants you to make the best appearance possible. They know you are under pressure – but they also want to see how you respond to it as a guide to what your reaction would be under the pressures of the job you seek. They will be influenced by the degree of poise you display, the personal traits you show and the manner in which you respond.

ABOUT THIS BOOK

This book contains tests divided into Examination Sections. Go through each test, answering every question in the margin. We have also attached a sample answer sheet at the back of the book that can be removed and used. At the end of each test look at the answer key and check your answers. On the ones you got wrong, look at the right answer choice and learn. Do not fill in the answers first. Do not memorize the questions and answers, but understand the answer and principles involved. On your test, the questions will likely be different from the samples. Questions are changed and new ones added. If you understand these past questions you should have success with any changes that arise. Tests may consist of several types of questions. We have additional books on each subject should more study be advisable or necessary for you. Finally, the more you study, the better prepared you will be. This book is intended to be the last thing you study before you walk into the examination room. Prior study of relevant texts is also recommended. NLC publishes some of these in our Fundamental Series. Knowledge and good sense are important factors in passing your exam. Good luck also helps. So now study this Passbook, absorb the material contained within and take that knowledge into the examination. Then do your best to pass that exam.

EXAMINATION SECTION

EXAMINATION SECTION
TEST 1

DIRECTIONS: Each question or incomplete statement is followed by several suggested answers or completions. Select the one that BEST answers the question or completes the statement. *PRINT THE LETTER OF THE CORRECT ANSWER IN THE SPACE AT THE RIGHT.*

1. The PRIMARY purpose of program analysis as it is used in government is to
    A. replace political judgments with rational programs and policies
    B. help decision-makers to sharpen their judgments about program choices
    C. analyze the impact of past programs on the quality of public services
    D. reduce costs by eliminating waste in public programs and services

1.____

2. While there is no complete method for program analysis that is agreed to by all the experts and is relevant to all types of problems, the MOST important element in program analysis involves the
    A. development of alternatives and the definition of objectives or criteria
    B. collection of information and the construction of a mathematical model
    C. design of experiments and procedures to validate results
    D. collection of expert opinion and the combination of their views

2.____

3. Electronic data processing is a particularly valuable tool of analysis in situations where the analyst has a processing problem involving
    A. *small* input, *few* operations, and *small* output
    B. *large* input, *many* operations, and *small* output
    C. *large* input, *few* operations, and *large* output
    D. *small* input, *many* operations, and *small* output

3.____

4. In order for an analyst to use electronic data processing to solve an analytic problem, the problem must be clearly defined.
The BEST way to prepare material for such definition in electronic data processing is to
    A. discuss the problem with computer programmers in a meeting
    B. prepare a flow diagram outlining the steps in the analysis
    C. write a memorandum with a list of the relevant program issues
    D. write a computer program using FORTRAN, BASIC, or another language

4.____

5. The "growth rate" referred to in current political and economic discussion refers to change from year to year in a country's
    A. investments   B. population
    C. gross national product D. sale of goods

5.____

6. Interactive or conversational programming is important to the program analyst ESPECIALLY for
   A. preparing analyses leading to management information systems
   B. communicating among analysts in different places
   C. using canned programs in statistical analysis
   D. testing trial solutions in rapid sequence

7. Program analysts often calls for recommendation of a choice between competing program possibilities that differ in the timing of major costs. Analysts using the present value technique by setting an interest or discount rate are in effect arguing that, other things being equal,
   A. it is inadvisable to defer the start of projects because of rising costs
   B. projects should be completed within a short time period to save money
   C. expenditures should be made out of tax revenues to avoid payment of interest
   D. postponing expenditures is advantageous at some measurable rate

8. Of the following, the formula which is MOST appropriately used to estimate the net need for a given type of service is that net need equals
   A. current clients – anticipate losses + anticipated gains
   B. $\frac{current\ supply}{standard}$ + current clients
   C. (client population x standard) – current supply
   D. current supply – anticipated losses + anticipated gains

9. The purpose of feasibility analysis is to protect the analyst from naïve alternatives and, MOST generally, to
   A. identify and quantify technological constraints
   B. carry out a preliminary stage of analysis
   C. anticipate potential blocks to implementation
   D. line up the support of political leadership

Questions 10-11.

DIRECTIONS: Questions 10 and 11 are to be answered on the basis of the following chart. In a hypothetical problem involving four criteria and four alternatives, the following data have been assembled.

Cost Criterion	Effectiveness Criterion	Timing Criterion	Feasibility Criterion
Alternative A $500,000	50 units	3 months	probably feasible
Alternative B $300,000	100 units	6 months	probably feasible
Alternative C $400,000	50 units	12 months	probably infeasible
Alternative D $200,000	75 units	3 months	probably infeasible

10. On the basis of the above data, it appears that the one alternative which is dominated by another alternative is Alternative
    A. A   B. B   C. C   D. D

11. If the feasibility constraint is absolute and fixed, then the critical trade-off is between lower cost
    A. on the one hand and faster timing and higher effectiveness on the other
    B. and higher effectiveness on one hand and faster timing on the other
    C. and faster timing on the one hand and higher effectiveness on the other
    D. on the one hand and higher effectiveness on the other

12. A classification of an agency's activities in a program structure is MOST useful if it highlights
    A. trade-offs that might not otherwise be considered
    B. ways to improve the efficiency of each activity
    C. the true organizational structure of an agency
    D. bases for insuring that expenditures stay within limits

13. CPM, like PERT, is a useful tool for scheduling large-scale, complex processes. In CPM, the critical path is the
    A. path composed of important links
    B. path composed of uncertain links
    C. longest path through the network
    D. shortest path through the network

14. Classical evaluative research calls for the use of control groups. However, there are practical difficulties in collecting data on individuals to be used as "controls" in program evaluations.
    Researchers may attempt to overcome these difficulties by
    A. using control groups that have no choice such as prison inmates or inmates of other public institutions or facilities
    B. developing better measures of the inputs, processes, and outputs relevant to public programs and services
    C. using experimental demonstration projects with participants in the different projects serving as comparison groups for one another
    D. abandoning attempts at formal evaluation in favor of more qualitative approaches employing a journalistic style of analysis

15. During the course of an analysis of the remaining "life" of a certain city's landfill for refuse disposal, there was a great deal of debate about the impact of changing rates of garbage generation on the amount of landfill needed and about what rates of garbage generation to expect over the next decade. Faced with the need to attempt to resolve this debate, an analyst would construct a simple model of the refuse disposal system and
    A. project landfill needs without considering refuse generation in the future
    B. conduct a detailed household survey in order to estimate future garbage generation rates
    C. ask the experts to continue to debate the issue until the argument is won by one view
    D. do a sensitivity analysis to test the impact of alternative assumptions about refuse generation

16. The limitations of traditional surveys have fostered the development and use of panels.
A panel is a
    A. group of respondents that serves as a continuous source of survey information
    B. group of advisors expert in the design and implementation of surveys
    C. representative sample of respondents at a single point in time
    D. post-survey discussion group composed of former respondents

17. The difference between sensitivity analysis and risk analysis is that risk analysis
    A. is applicable only to profit and loss situations where the concept of risk is operable
    B. includes an estimate of probabilities of different values of input factors
    C. is applicable to physical problems while sensitivity analysis is applicable to social ones
    D. requires a computer simulation while sensitivity analysis does not

18. A decision tree, although initially applied to business problems, is a graphic device which is useful to public analysts in
    A. scheduling complex processes
    B. doing long-range forecasting
    C. formulating the structure of alternatives
    D. solving production-inventory problems

19. The purpose of a management information system in an agency is to
    A. structure data relevant to managerial decision-making
    B. put all of an agency's data in machine-processing form
    C. simplify the record-keeping operations in an agency
    D. keep an ongoing record of management's activities

20.

    Assume that an analyst is presented with the above chart for a fire department and supplied also with information indicating a stable size firefighting staff over this time.
    The analyst could REASONABLY conclude regarding productivity that
    A. productivity over this time period was essentially stable for this firefighting force because the number of responses to real fires during this period was stable, as was the work force
    B. productivity was essentially increasing for this force because the number of total responses was increasing relative to a stable force

C. productivity was declining because a greater proportion of the total work effort was wasted effort in responding to false alarms
D. it is impossible to make a judgment about the productivity of the firefighting staff without a judgment about the value of a response to a false alarm

21. In the design of a productivity program for the sanitary department, the BEST measure of productivity would be
    A. tons of refuse collected annually
    B. number of collections made per week
    C. tons of refuse collected per truck shift
    D. number of trucks used per shift

    21.____

22. The cohort-survival method for estimating future population has been widely employed.
    In this method,
    A. migration is assumed to be constant over time
    B. net migration within cohorts is assumed to be zero
    C. migration is included as a multiplier factor
    D. net migration within cohorts is assumed to be constant

    22.____

23. Cost-effectiveness and cost-benefit analysis represent a systematic approach to balancing potential losses against potential gains as a prelude to public action.
    In addition to limitations based on difficulties of measurement and inadequacies in data that are typical of systematic program analysis, cost-benefit analysis suffers from a serious conceptual flaw in that
    A. the definition of benefit or cost does not typically distinguish to whom benefits or costs accrue
    B. a full-scale cost benefit analysis takes too long to do, is too expensive, and needs too much data
    C. it has been shown that such analyses are more suitable for defense or water resources problems
    D. such analyses are not useful in any problem involving capital and operating costs or benefits

    23.____

24. If you were asked to develop a total cost estimate for one year for a program involving both a capital improvement and operating costs, the BEST way to estimate the capital cost component would be to
    A. divide the estimated cost of the capital improvement by the projected operating costs over the life of the improvement
    B. multiply the annual operating cost by the projected life of the capital improvement
    C. divide the amortized cost of the capital improvement by the projected life of the improvement
    D. multiply the portion of the capital improvement to be completed within the year by the cost of the improvement

    24.____

25. In comparing the costs of two or more alternative programs, it is important to consider all relevant costs.
    The MOST important principle in defining "relevant cost" is that
    A. only marginal or incremental cost should be considered in the estimate
    B. only recurring costs should be considered for each alternative
    C. estimates should include the sunk costs for each alternative
    D. cost estimates need to be as precise as in budget preparation

26. Different techniques for projecting future costs may be suitable in different situations. Assume that it is necessary to estimate the future costs of maintaining garbage collection vehicles.
    Under which of the following conditions would it be advisable to develop a cost-estimating equation rather than to use unadjusted current data?
    A. When it is expected that more complex equipment will replace simpler equipment
    B. Whether or not it is expected that the nature of future garbage collection will change
    C. When the current unadjusted data still has to be verified
    D. When the nature of future garbage collection equipment is unknown

27. The following data has been collected on the costs of two pilot programs, each representing a different approach to the same problem.

	Total Cost	Fixed Cost	Variable Cost	Average Unit Cost	Number of Users
Program A	$45,000	$20,000	$50 per user	$90 Per User	500
Program B	$42,000	$7,000	$100 Per User	$120 Per User	350

    Assume that the pilot programs are extended city-wide and other factors are constant.
    Using the above data, what would a cost analysis conclude about the relative costs of the two programs?
    Program
    A. B would be less costly with fewer than 300 users and Program A would be less costly with more than 300 users
    B. B would be less costly with fewer than 260 users and Program A would be less costly with more than 260 users
    C. A would be less costly without regard to the size of the program
    D. B would be less costly without regard to the size of the program

Questions 28-30.

DIRECTIONS: Questions 28 through 30 are to be answered on the basis of the following data assembled for a cost-benefit analysis.

	Cost	Benefit
No program	0	0
Alternative W	$3,000	$6,000
Alternative X	$10,000	$17,000
Alternative Y	$17,000	$25,000
Alternative Z	$30,000	$32,000

28. From the point of view of pushing public expenditure to the point where marginal benefit equals or exceeds marginal cost, the BEST alternative is Alternative 28._____
    A. W   B. X   C. Y   D. Z

29. From the point of view of selecting the alternative with the best cost-benefit ratio, the BEST alternative is Alternative 29._____
    A. W   B. X   C. Y   D. Z

30. From the point of view of selecting the alternative with the best measure of net benefit, the BEST alternative is Alternative 30._____
    A. W   B. X   C. Y   D. Z

Questions 31-35.

DIRECTIONS: The set of answers listed below applies to Questions 31 through 35. Each answer is a type of statistical test.

   A. Analysis of variance
   B. Pearson Product-Moment Correlation (r)
   C. t-test
   D. x^2 test (Chi-squared)

   Pick the test which is MOST appropriate to the situation described. An answer may be used more than once.

31. A comparison between two correlated means obtained from a small sample. 31._____
    The CORRECT answer is:
    A. A   B. B   C. C   D. D

32. A comparison of three or more means. 32._____
    The CORRECT answer is:
    A. A   B. B   C. C   D. D

33. A comparison of the divergence of observed frequencies with those expected on the hypothesis of equal probability of occurrence. 33._____
    The CORRECT answer is:
    A. A   B. B   C. C   D. D

34. A comparison of the divergence of observed frequencies with those expected on the hypothesis of a normal distribution. 34._____
    The CORRECT answer is:
    A. A   B. B   C. C   D. D

35. A comparison between two uncorrelated means obtained from small samples. 35._____
    The CORRECT answer is:
    A. A   B. B   C. C   D. D

36. There are many different models for evaluative research.
A time-series design is an example of a _____ experimental design.
    A. field B. true C. quasi- D. pre-

37. In policy research, as in all kinds of research, it is important to develop research hypotheses early.
The MAIN purpose of a research hypothesis is to
    A. include the kind of statistical procedures to be used in the research
    B. provide a ready answer in case data is not available for doing research
    C. serve as a guide to the kind of data that must be collected in order to answer the research question
    D. clarify what is known and what is not known in the research problem

38. While descriptive and causal research are not completely separable, there has been a distinct effort to move in the direction of causal research.
Such an effort is epitomized by the use of
    A. predictive models and measures of deviation from predictions
    B. option and attitudinal surveys in local neighborhoods
    C. community studies and area profiles of localities
    D. individual case histories and group case studies

39. The one of the following which BEST describes a periodic report is that it
    A. provides a record of accomplishments for a given time span and a comparison with similar time spans in the past
    B. covers the progress made in a project that has been postponed
    C. integrates, summarizes, and perhaps interprets published data on technical or scientific material
    D. describes a decision, advocates a policy or action, and presents facts in support of the writer's position

40. The PRIMARY purpose of including pictorial illustrations in a formal report is usually to
    A. amplify information which has been adequately treated verbally
    B. present detail that are difficult to describe verbally
    C. provide the reader with a pleasant, momentary distraction
    D. present supplementary information incidental to the main ideas developed in the report

KEY (CORRECT ANSWERS)

1.	B	11.	B	21.	C	31.	C
2.	A	12.	A	22.	B	32.	A
3.	B	13.	C	23.	A	33.	D
4.	B	14.	C	24.	C	34.	D
5.	C	15.	D	25.	A	35.	C
6.	D	16.	A	26.	A	36.	C
7.	D	17.	B	27.	B	37.	C
8.	C	18.	C	28.	C	38.	A
9.	C	19.	A	29.	A	39.	A
10.	C	20.	D	30.	C	40.	B

TEST 2

DIRECTIONS: Each question or incomplete statement is followed by several suggested answers or completions. Select the one that BEST answers the question or completes the statement. *PRINT THE LETTER OF THE CORRECT ANSWER IN THE SPACE AT THE RIGHT.*

1. A measurement procedure is considered to be RELIABLE to the extent that 1.____
   A. independent applications under similar conditions yield consistent results
   B. independent applications under different conditions yield similar results
   C. scores reflect true differences among individuals or situations
   D. scores reflect true differences in the same individual over time

2. Different scales of measurement are distinguished by the feasibility of various empirical operations. 2.____
   An ordinal scale of measurement
   A. is not as useful as a ratio or interval scale
   B. is useful in rank-ordering or priority setting
   C. provides the data for addition or subtraction
   D. provides the data for computation of means

3. A widely used approach to sampling is systematic sampling, i.e., selecting every Kth element in a listing. 3.____
   Even with a random start, a DISADVANTAGE in this approach is that
   A. the listing used may contain a cyclical pattern
   B. it is too similar to a simple random sample
   C. the system does not insure a probability sample
   D. it yield an unpredictable sample size

4. A rule of thumb sometimes used in sample size selection it to set sample size equal to five percent of the population size. 4.____
   Other things being equal, this rule
   A. tends to oversample small populations
   B. tends to oversample large populations
   C. provides an accurate rule for sampling
   D. is a relatively inexpensive basis for sampling

5. With regard to a stratified random sample, it may be APPROPRIATE to sample the various strata in different proportions in order to 5.____
   A. approximate the characteristics of a true random sample
   B. establish classes that are internally heterogenous in each case
   C. avoid the necessity of subdividing the cases within each stratum
   D. adequately cover important strata that have small numbers of cases

6. One possible response to the "unknown" or "no answer" category in a tabulation of survey information is to "allocate" the unknown responses, i.e., to estimate the missing data on the basis of other known information about the respondents. 6.____

This technique is APPROPRIATE when the unknown category
- A. is very small and is randomly distributed within all subgroups of respondents
- B. is very large and is randomly distributed within all subgroups of respondents
- C. reflects an interviewing failure and a subgroup in the sample ends to produce more unknowns
- D. is a legitimate category and a subgroup in the sample tends to produce more unknowns

7. In presenting cross-tabulated data showing the relationship between two variables, it is MOST meaningful to compute percentages
   - A. in both directions in all instances
   - B. of each cell in relation to the grand total
   - C. in the direction of the smaller number of cells
   - D. in the direction of the causal factor

8. In portraying data based on a sampling operation, it is MOST meaningful and comprehensible to the reader to present
   - A. percentages for the sample and the universe
   - B. percentages by themselves
   - C. percentages and the base figures
   - D. numbers by themselves

9. A new bridge spanning a river is expected to carry 60,000 cars a day on a rainy day and 80,000 cars a day on other kinds of days.
   If there is a $5 toll and one chance in four of a rainy day, the expected value of a day's revenue is
   - A. $175,000
   - B. $375,000
   - C. $475,000
   - D. $700,000

10. The analyst who is asked to estimate the probability of a relatively rare event occurring cannot use the classical frequency measures of probability but rather should
    - A. use a random-numbers table to pick a probability
    - B. project historical data into the future
    - C. indicate that no probabilistic judgment is possible
    - D. make the best possible judgment as to the subjective probability

11. A useful source of census data for computing annual indicators is the
    - A. Public Use Sample
    - B. Continuing Population Survey
    - C. Census of Population
    - D. Census of Governments

12. An analyst presented with a set of household records showing age, ethnicity, income, and family status and wishing to study the inter-relationship of all of these variables simultaneously will probably equal
    - A. one four-way cross-tabulation
    - B. four three-way cross-tabulation
    - C. six two-way cross-tabulations
    - D. four single tabulations

13. Downward communication, from high management to lower levels in an organization, will often not be fully accepted at the lowest levels of an organization unless high-level management
    A. communicates through several levels of mid-level management, where the message can be properly modified and interpreted
    B. communicates directly with the level of the organization it wishes to reach, bypassing any intermediate levels
    C. first establishes an atmosphere in which upward communication is encouraged and listened to
    D. establishes penalties for non-compliance with its communications

13.____

14. A top-level manager sometimes has an inaccurate view of the actual lower-level operations of his agency, particularly of those operations which are not running well.
    Of the following, the MOST frequent cause of this is the
    A. general unconcern of top-level management with the way an agency actually operates
    B. tendency of the people at the lowest level in an agency to lie about their actual performance
    C. unwillingness of top-level management to deal with unfavorable information when it is presented
    D. tendency of mid-level management to edit bad news and unpleasant information from reports directed to top management

14.____

15. In the conduct of productivity analyses, work measurement is a USEFUL technique for
    A. substantiating executive decisions
    B. designing a research study
    C. developing performance yardsticks
    D. preparing a manual of procedure

15.____

16. Issue analysis is closely identified with the "fire-fighting" function of management. As such, issue analysis is a(n)
    A. systematic assessment over time of an agency's strategic options
    B. annual review of the issues that have come up during the past year
    C. basis for a set of procedures to be followed in an emergency
    D. analysis of a specific policy question often performed in a crisis environment

16.____

17. The transportation agency in a large city wishes to study the impact of fare increases on ridership in buses. Ridership data for peak hours has been assembled for the same time period for three geographic subareas (A, B, and C) with approximately the same socio-economic characteristics, residential density, and distance from the central business district (CBD). Subarea A had experienced a moderate fare increase on its bus line; Subarea B had had no fare increase; and Subarea C had experienced a major fare increase during the time period

17.____

In the design of this study, the analysis should be framed:
A. Ridership = f (fare level)
B. Ridership = f (fare level), distance from CBD)
C. Fare level = f (ridership)
D. Ridership = f (fare level, socio-economic characteristics, residential density)

18. What organizational concept is illustrated when a group is organized on an *ad hoc* basis to accomplish a specific goal?
    A. Functional Teamwork
    B. Line/staff
    C. Task Force
    D. Command

19. The concept of "demand" provides an appropriate theoretical basis for estimating the needs for public services or programs where the service will be on a _____ basis and _____ life-sustaining necessities.
    A. fee; involves
    B. free; involves
    C. free; does not involve
    D. fee; does not involve

20. Analysts should be wary of relying exclusively on traditional service standards (e.g., one acre of playground per 1,000 population).
    Such standards are often DEFICIENT because they tend to overstate
    A. the consumer view and understate behavior and values of producers
    B. the producer view and understate behavior and values of users or consumers
    C. local conditions and understate national conditions
    D. behavioral factors and understate practical effects

21. The BEST measure of the performance of a manpower program would be
    A. percentage reduction in unemployment by impacted population groups
    B. number of trainees placed in jobs at the beginning of the training program
    C. percentage of students completing a training program
    D. cost per student of the training program and the job placement effort

22. Indices are single figures that measure multi-dimensional concepts.
    The critical judgment in the construction of an index involves
    A. the trade-off between accuracy and simplicity
    B. determination of enough data to do the measurement
    C. avoidance of all possible error
    D. developing a theoretical basis for it

23. Evaluation of public programs is complicated by the reality that programs tend to reflect negotiated compromises among conflicting objectives.
    The absence of clear, unitary objectives PARTICULARLY complicates the
    A. assessment of program input or effort
    B. development of effectiveness criteria
    C. design of new programs to replace the old
    D. diagnosis of a program's processes

5 (#2)

24. The BASIC purpose of the "Super-Agencies" is to
    A. reduce the number of departments and agencies in the city government
    B. reduce the number of high-level administrators
    C. coordinate agencies reporting to the mayor and supervise agencies in related fields
    D. supervise departments and agencies in unrelated fields

25. In most municipal budgeting systems involving capital and operating budgets, the leasing or renting of facilities is usually shown in
    A. the operating budget   B. the capital budget
    C. a separate schedule   D. either budget

26. New York City's budgeting procedure is unusual in that budget appropriations are considered in two parts, as follows:
    A. Capital budget and income budget
    B. Expense budget and income budget
    C. Revenue budget and expense budget
    D. Expense budget and capital budget

27. The "growth rate" referred to in current political and economic discussion refers to change from year to year in a country's
    A. gross national product   B. population
    C. available labor force   D. capital goods investment

Questions 28-29.

DIRECTIONS: Questions 28 and 29 are to be answered on the basis of the following illustration. Assume that the figures in the chart are cubes.

28. In the illustration above, how many times GREATER is the quantity represented by Figure III than the quantity represented by Figure II?
    A. 2   B. 4   C. 8   D. 16

29. The above illustration illustrates a progression in quantity BEST described as
    A. arithmetic   B. geometric   C. discrete   D. linear

Questions 30-35.

DIRECTIONS: Questions 30 through 35 are to be answered on the basis of the following chart.

In a national study of poverty trends, the following data have been assembled by interpretation.

Persons Below Poverty, By Residence				
	Number (millions)		Percent	
Item	U.S.	Metropolitan Areas	U.S.	Metropolitan Areas
2010				
Total	38.8	17.0	22.0	15.3
Under 25 years	20.0	8.8	25.3	18.1
65 years & over	5.5	2.5	35.2	26.9
Black	9.9	5.0	55.1	42.8
Other	28.3	11.8	18.1	12.0
2020				
Total	24.3	12.3	12.2	9.5
Under 25 years	12.2	6.4	13.2	10.4
65 years & over	4.8	2.3	25.3	20.2
Black	7.2	3.9	32.3	24.4
Other	16.7	8.2	9.5	7.3

30. If no other source of data were available, which of the following groups would you expect to have the HIGHEST rate of poverty?
    A. Others over 65
    B. Others under 65
    C. Blacks over 65
    D. Blacks under 65

30.____

31. Between 2010 and 2020, the percentage of poor in the United States who were Black
    A. increased from 25.5% to 29.6%
    B. decreased from 55.1% to 32.3%
    C. decreased from 9.9% to 7.2%
    D. stayed the same

31.____

32. The data in the second column of the table indicate that, in the metropolitan areas, the number of poor declined by 4.7 million or 36.2% between 2010 and 2020. Yet, the fourth column shows a corresponding decline from 15.3% to 9.5%, or only 5.8%.
    This apparent discrepancy reflects the fact that
    A. metropolitan areas are growing while the number of poor is contracting
    B. two columns in question are based on different sources of information
    C. difference between two percentages is not the same as the percent change in total numbers
    D. tables have inherent errors and must be carefully checked

32.____

33. The percentages in each of the last two columns of the table for 2010 and 2020 don't add up to 100%. This is for the reason that
    A. rounding off each entry to the nearest decimal place caused an error in the total such that the total is not equal to 100%
    B. these columns show the percentage of Blacks, aged, etc. who are poor rather than the percentage of poor who are Black, aged, etc.
    C. there was an error in the construction of the table which was not noticed until the table was already in print
    D. there is double counting in the entries in the table; some people ae counted more than once

34. Data such as that presented in the table on persons below poverty level are shown to a single decimal place because
    A. data in every table should always be shown to a single decimal place
    B. it is the minimal number of decimal places needed to distinguish among table entries
    C. there was no room for more decimal places in the table without crowding
    D. the more accurately a figure is shown the better it is for the user

35. In comparing the poverty of the young (under 25 years) with that of the older population (65 years and over) in 2010 and 2020, one could REASONABLY conclude that
    A. more young people than old people were poor but older people had a higher rate of poverty
    B. more older people than young people were poor but young people had a higher rate of poverty
    C. there is a greater degree of poverty among the younger population than among the older people

Questions 36-37.

DIRECTIONS: Questions 36 and 37 are to be answered ONLY on the basis of the information given in the following passage.

Two approaches are available in developing criteria for the evaluation of plans. One approach, designated Approach A, is a review and analysis of characteristics that differentiate successful plans from unsuccessful plans. These criteria are descriptive in nature and serve as a checklist against which the plan under consideration may be judged. These characteristics have been observed by many different students of planning, and there is considerable agreement concerning the characteristics necessary for a plan to be successful.
A second approach to the development of criteria for judging plans, designated Approach B is the determination of the degree to which the plan under consideration is economic. The word "economic" is used here in its broadest sense, i.e., effective in its utilization of resources. In order to determine the economic worth of a plan, it is necessary to use a technique that permits the description of any plan in economic terms and to utilize this technique to the extent that it becomes a "way of thinking" about plans.

36. According to Approach B, the MOST successful plan is generally one which
    A. costs least to implement
    B. gives most value for resources expended
    C. uses the least expensive resources
    D. utilizes the greatest number of resources

37. According to Approach A, a successful plan is one which is
    A. descriptive in nature
    B. lowest in cost
    C. similar to other successful plans
    D. agreed upon by many students of planning

Questions 38-40.

DIRECTIONS: Questions 38 through 40 are to be answered ONLY on the basis of the information provided in the following passage.

The primary purpose of control reports is to supply information intended to serve as the basis for corrective action if needed. At the same time, the significance of control reports must be kept in proper perspective. Control reports are only a part of the planning-management information system. Control information includes non-financial as well as financial data that measure performance and isolate variances from standard. Control information also provides feedback so that planning information may be updated and corrected. Whenever possible, control reports should be designed so that they provide feedback for the planning process as well as provide information of immediate value to the control process.

Since the culmination of the control process is the taking of necessary corrective action to bring performance in line with standards, it follows that control information must be directed to the person who is organizationally responsible for taking the required action. Usually the same information, though in a somewhat abbreviated form, is given to the responsible manager's superior. A district sales manager needs a complete daily record of the performance of each of his salesmen; yet, the report forwarded to the regional sales manager summarizes only the performance of each sales district in his region. In preparing reports for higher echelons of management, summary statements and recommendations for action should appear on the first page; substantiating data, usually the information presented to the person directly responsible for the operation, may be include if needed.

38. A control report serves its primary purpose as part of the process which leads DIRECTLY to
    A. better planning for future action
    B. increasing the performance of district salesmen
    C. the establishment of proper performance standards
    D. taking corrective action when performance is poor

39. The one of the following which would be the BEST description of a control report is that a control report is a form of
    A. planning   B. communication
    C. direction   D. organization

40. If control reports are to be effective, the one of the following which is LEAST essential to the effectiveness of control reporting is a system of
    A. communication
    B. standards
    C. authority
    D. work simplification

KEY (CORRECT ANSWERS)

1.	A	11.	B	21.	A	31.	B
2.	B	12.	A	22.	A	32.	C
3.	A	13.	C	23.	B	33.	B
4.	B	14.	D	24.	C	34.	D
5.	D	15.	C	25.	A	35.	A
6.	C	16.	D	26.	D	36.	B
7.	D	17.	A	27.	A	37.	C
8.	C	18.	C	28.	C	38.	D
9.	B	19.	D	29.	B	39.	B
10.	D	20.	B	30.	C	40.	D

EXAMINATION SECTION
TEST 1

DIRECTIONS: Each question or incomplete statement is followed by several suggested answers or completions. Select the one that *BEST* answers the question or completes the statement. *PRINT THE LETTER OF THE CORRECT ANSWER IN THE SPACE AT THE RIGHT.*

1. An analyst is writing a report dealing with the distribution of deaths caused by various types of cardiovascular diseases. He decides to facilitate the reader's grasp of the information presented by including in the report a device that permits comparison of parts to each other, and to the whole at the same time.
   Of the following, the *MOST* appropriate and efficient device he should use for this purpose is the

   A. graph
   B. pie diagram
   C. flow sheet
   D. line chart with one series

   1.____

2. In carrying out a cost-effectiveness analysis, the analyst should follow certain guidelines. The *MOST* important of these guidelines involves the

   A. utilization of both the fixed utility approach and the fixed budget approach
   B. proper structuring of the problem and design of the analysis
   C. necessity of building a model that is highly formal and mathematical
   D. provision for implicit treatment of uncertainty

   2.____

3. In a decision which involves fairness -- such as assigning new office equipment to workers when the agency does not receive enough new office equipment for the entire group -- the *PRIMARY* determinant of the decision's effectiveness will be the

   A. systematic or traditional approach which is emphasized in reaching the decision
   B. random nature of the assignment
   C. feedback a decisionmaker receives concerning the decision
   D. acceptance of the decision by the persons who have to execute it

   3.____

4. In order to give line personnel some insight into staff problems and vice versa it has been suggested that line and staff assignments within a particular city agency be rotated. Which of the following criticisms would be *MOST* valid for opposing such a proposal?

   A. Generally speaking, line and staff personnel have different perspectives on organizational structures which makes rotation in assignments extremely difficult.
   B. Since their educational backgrounds are often quite diverse, staff personnel are often at a disadvantage when serving in line assignments.
   C. Line personnel frequently resent having to perform the more difficult tasks that staff assignments entail.
   D. Serving in a rotating assignment may not necessarily provide the personnel with any significant degree of insight as anticipated.

   4.____

5. Which one of the following approaches to criticism of a subordinate or associate is *generally* the *MOST* appropriate and effective?
   Criticize

   A. by making a comparison with a more exemplary employee

   5.____

B. the act, not the person
C. in a humorous vein
D. in general rather than specific terms

6. Assume that two policy units have been formed to study the impact of Federal programs in the city. The two units operate in an essentially similar manner, except for their communications procedures. In unit A any member may communicate and exchange information with any other member of the unit; in unit B a member may only communicate information with the unit supervisor.
In evaluating the effect that these communications procedures have on the level of productivity, it will *generally* be found that

   A. unit A's level of productivity will be greater than unit B's level of productivity for simple problems
   B. unit B's level of productivity will be greater than unit A's level of productivity for simple problems
   C. initial levels of profuctivity are higher in unit A than unit B for complex problems
   D. initial levels of productivity are higher in unit B than in unit A for complex problems

7. In the process of communicating an idea, the following five distinct steps are generally involved:
   I. Selection of a media and transmission of the message
   II. Decoding of a message, i.e., meaning is extracted from the message
   III. Message is received
   IV. Idea is organized into a series of symbols designed to give meaning
   V. Action is taken and/or feedback is given

   In what logical, sequential order should these steps be arranged for effective two-way communications to take place?

   A. V, I, II, III, IV
   B. II, I, III, IV, V
   C. IV, I, III, II, V
   D. I, III, IV, II, V

8. Informal employee groups that share certain norms and strive for member satisfaction through the achievement of group goals are known as work groups.
Which of the following statements can *generally* be considered as being *FALSE* in describing work groups in a moderate size organization?

   A. Formation of work groups is ubiquitous and inevitable.
   B. Work groups strongly influence the overall behavior and performance of their members.
   C. An organization can reap positive and negative consequences as a result of work groups.
   D. Elimination of work groups can be easily achieved by management pressure.

9. Under the management approach known as *management by objectives* which of the following criteria is *generally* used to determine whether the manager has been successful?

   A. Activities performed
   B. Results achieved
   C. Production schedules completed
   D. Financial savings accomplished

10. Of the following, the MOST accurate statement relative to job attitudes is that they

    A. cannot be influenced by only one person
    B. are always the result of work groups
    C. have no relationship to productivity
    D. are strongly influenced by work situation

11. Assume that measures to overcome a budget deficit, including attrition and a hiring freeze, have significantly decreased the work-output of a city agency. The agency administrator desires to develop a plan to restore production to its former level by increasing the work-load and responsibility of the agency's employees.
    In order to obtain *maximum* employee cooperation and *minimize* employee resistance, it would be MOST advisable for the

    A. administrator of the agency to personally describe to the employees the new work changes that they are to follow
    B. employees to decide what the optimal changes in the work load should be
    C. management representatives to consult with employee representatives on these matters
    D. immediate supervisor of the employees to decide on the work changes to be implemented

12. Eliciting the support and cooperation of others often requires a great deal of persuasion. Which one of the following persuasive techniques or practices is generally the LEAST desirable for you, an analyst, to use?

    A. Establish your expertness and authority
    B. Present your arguments without emotion
    C. In presenting your arguments, express yourself in the manner to which you are accustomed
    D. Try to find a face-saving way for your opponent to change his/her mind

13. The following illustration depicts the structure of a municipal agency.

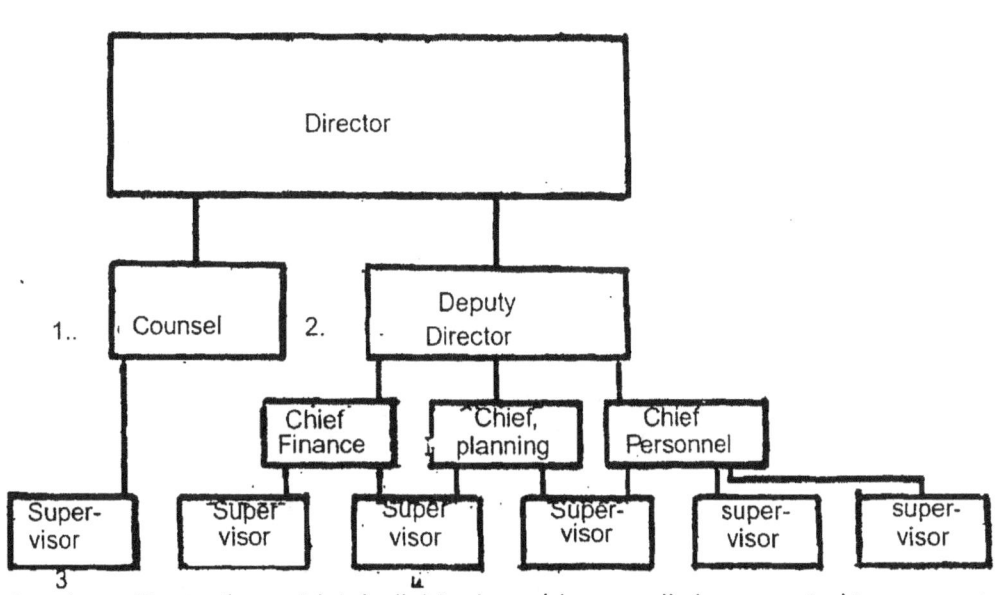

In the above illustration, which individual would generally be expected to encounter the MOST difficulty in carrying out his organizational functions?

    A. 1   B. 2   C. 3   D. 4

14. An agency in which a free flow of communication exists is an agency in which no barriers or structures are erected to control or bar the flow of information and messages between and among management and staff, horizontally or vertically.
    Of the following, the GREATEST disadvantage that would be most likely to occur in an agency in which such a free flow of communication exists, is that

    A. it would be difficult to determine which information is important and which is irrelevant
    B. there would be a lesser degree of staff-employee participation and cooperation in communicating
    C. more restrictive controls would be placed on managerial employees
    D. important communications would tend to be eliminated, and and trivial communications over-emphasized

15. Feedback is generally considered an essential factor in oral communication MAINLY because

    A. it enables the speaker to know whether he is understood
    B. the speed of communication is accelerated
    C. it eliminates the necessity of the speaker to use gestures and facial expressions when speaking
    D. the listener is unable to immediately respond to the speaker until the latter is finished

16. Assume that two employees are working on a joint project and they have a difference of opinion on the methodology to be used. Each employee not only listens to the other's opinion on methodology but projects him-self into the other's position.
    This type of listening is *usually* considered

    A. *ineffective*, mainly because it will be impossible for the employees to reach a satisfactory agreement
    B. *effective*, mainly because each employee will then be more critical of the other's argument
    C. *ineffective*, mainly because each worker will unconsciously and unintentionally accept the other's viewpoint
    D. *effective*, mainly because each speaker can understand the other's viewpoint and can then respond intelligently to his remarks

17. The arithmetic mean is commonly used in describing data. Which one of the following statements is NOT true about the arithmetic mean?

    A. It is a measure of dispersion.
    B. The sum of the deviations around it is zero.
    C. It is easy to compute, understand and recognize.
    D. It may be treated alegebraically.

Questions 18 - 20.

DIRECTIONS: Answer Questions 18 through 20 on the basis of the following data. Assume that you are using these data in assessing the impact of Federal and State income taxes on New York City residents, and comparing it to the effect of Federal and State taxes in other areas.

EFFECT OF DEDUCTIBILITY (i.e., deductibility of taxes levied by other jurisdictions in calculating the net base of the tax in the taxing jurisdiction.)

Net income before personal exemption	Effective rate of tax				
	Federal (assuming no state tax)	State		Combined Federal and State	
		New York*	Minnesota (assuming no federal tax)	New York	Minnesota
	(1)	(2)	(3)	(4)	(5)
$20,000	25.0	4.1	6.9	27.6	27.9
50,000	42.2	5.4	9.1	44.0	43.9
100,000	56.0	5.9	9.8	57.5	57.1
200,000	69.2	6.1	10.1	69.9	69.5
1,500,000	88.0	6.3	10.5	89.3	88.9

*New York has no deductibility; the Federal government has deductibility.

18. In which of the following columns is the tax rate shown to be the *LEAST* progressive?   18._____

    A. 1   B. 2   C. 4   D. 5

19. Which of the following statements is *TRUE* about the reasons why Columns 1 and 2 do not equal Column 4 for each salary level?   19._____

    A. Personal deductions are taken into account in Column 4 but not in Columns 1 and 2.
    B. Federal deducibility of state taxes only is taken into account in Column 4 but not in Columns 1 and 2.
    C. Reciprocal deductibility is taken into account in Column 4 but not in Columns 1 and 2.
    D. State deductibility of federal taxes only is taken into account in Column 4 but not in Columns 1 and 2.

20. The *EFFECT* of the State's introducing deductibility, given that the Federal government maintains deductibility, is to   20._____

    A. *increase* Federal and State income
    B. *decrease* Federal and State income
    C. *decrease* Federal income and increase State income
    D. *increase* Federal income and decrease State income

21. Assume that you have been made project coordinator for a study concerning the implementation of casino gambling in the city. You have assigned each of the professional staff members simple tasks in specialized areas for the duration of the project. For you to make such job assignments would *generally* be

    A. *desirable;* the performance of simple tasks will motivate individuals to work diligently
    B. *desirable;* specialized tasks induce a sense of accomplishment to individuals
    C. *undesirable;* specialized tasks are more difficult to learn
    D. *undesirable;* specialized tasks may lead to a loss of feeling of accomplishment

22. Assume that you have been asked to submit a proposal for the reorganization of a unit that is charged with performing difficult nonroutine work. Frequently decisions must be made quickly and concurrence obtained from high-level agency heads.
    Given the above conditions, of the following it would be *MOST* logical to structure the organization

    A. on the basis of a relatively wide span of control
    B. on the basis of a relatively narrow span of control
    C. with many organizational levels with a wide span of control
    D. with more emphasis on line than staff units

23. Assume that a study has indicated that a recently created city *superagency* has had formal communication difficulties among various component agencies. It appears that jurisdictional overlapping among those agencies has caused frequent rerouting and unnecessary duplication of communications within the organization. Which one of the following proposals would *MOST* effectively deal with the communications problem encountered by this *superagency*?

    A. Create a central communications office to handle all communications for this *superagency.*
    B. Duplicate and distribute all communications to each component within this *superagency.*
    C. Reduce the overlapping areas of jurisdiction among the component agencies
    D. Decentralize the *superagency* on a *borough* basis to expedite mail delivery

24. The utilization of input-output concepts in connection with the application of the systems concept to government raises the problem of the quantification of objectives and performance (the value of the public benefit). The one of the following which is *MOST* easily *quantifiable* is

    A. education
    B. police service
    C. subway car maintenance
    D. the effectiveness of a welfare administrator

25. When an analyst tries to conceive of a city management problem as a *systems* problem, he is, first of all, confronted with establishing the boundaries of the system. Of the following, the city problem which can *most likely* be conceived of within a system whose boundaries are roughly equivalent to those of the city is

    A. taxation
    B. welfare
    C. fire protection
    D. transportation

25.____

KEY (CORRECT ANSWERS)

1.	B	11.	C
2.	B	12.	B
3.	D	13.	D
4.	D	14.	A
5.	B	15.	A
6.	C	16.	D
7.	C	17.	A
8.	D	18.	B
9.	B	19.	B
10.	D	20.	D

21. D
22. B
23. C
24. C
25. C

TEST 2

DIRECTIONS: Each question or incomplete statement is followed by several suggested answers or completions. Select the one that BEST answers the question or completes the statement. PRINT THE LETTER OF THE CORRECT ANSWER IN THE SPACE AT THE RIGHT.

1. When installing a new *system*, an analyst may choose among several types of installation plans - the *all-at-once type,* the *piecemeal type,* or the *parallel type* each suited to a particular problem or degree of complexity in the system.
   The one of the following situations in which the *parallel type* would be MOST appropriate is a situation

   A. in which a minimum installation cost is required
   B. involving a small volume of transactions
   C. in which the change is not radical or does not involve new machines
   D. involving large installation projects and intricate processing

   1.____

2. Many decision situations involve a great deal of uncertainty about the future, which is difficult to take into account in the analysis of alternatives. One technique developed for treating such uncertainty is designed to measure the possible effects on alternatives under analysis resulting from variations in uncertain elements. The analyst uses several *expected values* for uncertain parameters in an attempt to ascertain how the results vary (i.e., the relative ranking of the alternatives under consideration) in light of variations in the uncertain parameters. The analyst attempts to determine the alternative (or feasible combination of alternatives) likely to achieve a specified objective, gain or utility at the lowest cost. The one of the following which BEST describes the above technique is:

   A. Contingency analysis employing the fixed-budget approach
   B. Contingency analysis employing the fixed-benefits approach
   C. Sensitivity analysis employing the fixed-budget approach
   D. Sensitivity analysis employing the fixed-benefits approach

   2.____

3. In general, the analytical techniques of management science are of the LEAST value when

   A. the effects of a small number of controlled variables must be considered
   B. the number of relevant uncontrolled variables is small
   C. relevant causes and effects are factual in nature and can be stated and measured numerically or symbolically
   D. There are reasons to believe that past relationships will continue to hold in the future

   3.____

4. During the installation period of a new system, tight controls must be maintained over every phase of the operation. To do this, an analyst may set up a *warning system* within the system which forecasts potential bottle-necks and affords sufficient clues for correcting any problems, errors or fall-downs.
   The one of the following control devices or techniques which would be *most likely* to involve extra effort during the installation, and slow down the processing time is

   4.____

A. paper flow controls - log sheets, numerical controls, etc. (a system of logging input and output)
B. timing controls - to inform the analyst about the proper time interval between certain activities with-in the systems
C. program check points - a periodic review of processing to date at each check point
D. accounting control totals, to accumulate invoice numbers as the first and last steps in the system and compare the totals

5. Which of the following types of work measurement techniques would be MOST appropriate for obtaining details of a particular job for cost analysis purposes, such as the operating costs of various types of duplicating machines?

    A. Work sampling
    B. Predetermined time standards
    C. The time study (stop-watch timing)
    D. Historical

6. It is anticipated that a certain cancer detection program will be capable of detecting many cases at an early stage and that society will be thus enabled to cure twice as many cases as it cures currently. The benefits to society include the reduction in cost of hospitalization, etc., that would have been incurred otherwise.
Benefits such as a reduction in the cost of hospitalization are *most usually* called

    A. direct benefits
    B. secondary benefits
    C. intergenerational benefits
    D. external benefits

7. The results of departmental and agency programs can be measured in terms of *EFFECTIVENESS* or *BENEFITS*. Thus, careful budget preparation will permit the calculation of costs which can then be compared, or equated, to these results. Which one of the following statements pertaining to cost-effectiveness measurements is MOST valid?

    A. In cost-effectiveness measurements, a dollar value is assigned to the output.
    B. The measurement is expressed in terms of quality of output for a given cost.
    C. Cost effectiveness ratios express the relationship between the costs of programs
    D. A cost-effectiveness measurement will show the number of outputs which can be achieved for the expenditure of a given amount of money.

8. Assume that you have been asked to evaluate personnel programs in four city agencies The statistical test that would be MOST appropriate for testing the significance of the differences in the mean number of days absent (normality may be assumed) during the year 2004 in four different agencies is the

    A. one-way analysis of variance
    B. standard deviation
    C. regression analysis
    D. Chi-square test (x^2-test)

9. Assume that you have been asked to evaluate differences in the children just enrolled in two youth programs. In reviewing the relevant published material you find that in one particular study involving two groups, N = 9 and N = 13, there is a significant difference in the mean scores of the two groups on a characteristic which you believe to be normally distributed.
   The statistical test *most likely* used in this study to determine the significance of the difference in the means of the two groups on this characteristic is the

   A. Chi-square test (x2-test)
   B. Pearson Product-Moment correlation (r)
   C. t-test
   D. two-way analysis of variance

10. In statistics, three common measures of central tendency are the mean, median and mode.
    For which of the following conditions would the median generally be the *BEST* choice to use? When the

    A. distribution of scores is skewed
    B. scores are distributed symmetrically around a central point
    C. standard deviation must also be calculated
    D. most frequently occurring value is required

11. Nonparametric statistical tests are *usually* employed when

    A. large samples are used
    B. a very powerful or exact test is needed
    C. data cannot be expressed in ranks
    D. a normally distributed population cannot be assumed

12. Assume that in a report presented to you by an employee under your supervision, a coefficient of correlation of +1.73 is reported between the age at which one first smokes cigarettes and the age at which one first smokes marijuana.
    You should *most reasonably* interpret this figure to mean there is a

    A. strong positive correlation
    B. weak positive correlation
    C. weak negative correlation
    D. typographical error

13. One of the major research techniques most often used in studies of organizational behavior problems is the survey. An analyst who utilizes the survey technique should be aware that its *MAJOR* drawback is

    A. the lack of depth obtained from the two major data-collection tolls used in surveys: the mailed question-naire and the personal interview
    B. its impracticality in assessing or estimating the present state of affairs with regard to a variable that changes over time for a large group of subjects
    C. the restriction of this technique to a single, or very few, units of analysis
    D. its absence of dependence upon the collection of empirical data

14. In order for an analyst to understand and interpret statistical data he/she must understand which types of data tend to approximate the normal probability curve, i.e., are normally distributed.
Which of the following types of data falls into this category?
Frequency of

    A. educational test scores for students of a given age, plotted against test score
    B. filing of income tax returns for citizens of a given age, plotted against date of filing
    C. deaths due to childhood disease plotted against age
    D. deaths due to degenerative diseases, plotted against age

15. Which of the following terms describes a line or curve formed by plotting employees salaries that increase yearly by a fixed percentage over the previous year? (In answering the question, assume that time is on the horizontal axis (abscissa) and salary is on the vertical axis (ordinate) - both axes are marked linearly.)

    A. Linear (increasing at a constant rate)
    B. Positively accelerating (increasing at an increasing rate)
    C. Negatively accelerating (increasing at a decreasing rate)
    D. Negatively decelerating (decreasing at a decreasing rate)

Questions 16 - 17

DIRECTIONS: Answer Questions 16 and 17 on the basis of the following groups, both of which depict the same information in different ways.

The x and y axes in graphs A and B are not necessarily drawn in the same scale. The points along the curves on both graphs represent corresponding points, and are the upper limits of class intervals.

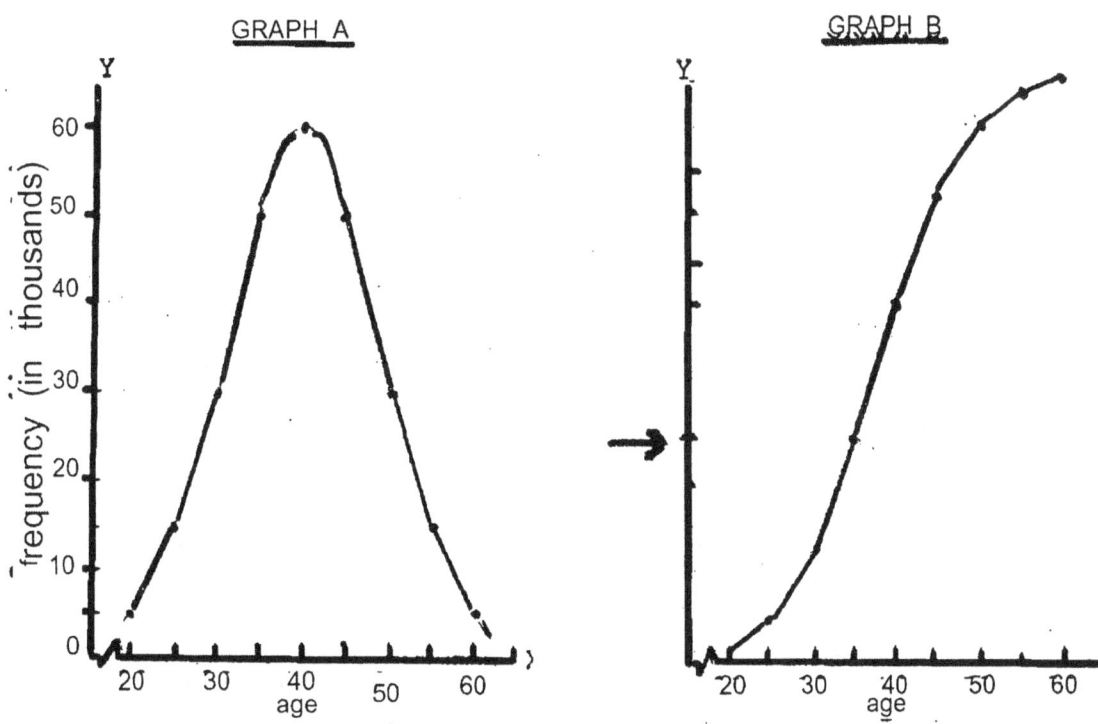

16. The ordinate (y-axis) in graph B is

    A. frequency
    B. cumulative frequency
    C. average frequency
    D. log frequency

17. The arrow on the y-axis in graph B indicates a particular number. That number is, *most nearly*

    A. 100 B. 50,000 C. 100,000 D. 150,000

Questions 18 - 19

DIRECTIONS: Answer Questions 18 and 19 on the basis of the graphs that appear on the following page.

18. In Graph I, the vertical distance between lines E and T within the crosshatched area represents the

    A. savings to the city if work of less than 50 miles is performed by the city
    B. loss to the city if work of less than 50 miles is performed by the city
    C. savings to the city if work of more than 50 miles is performed by the city
    D. loss to the city if work of more than 50 miles is performed by the city

19. Graph II is identical to Graph I except that contractor costs have been eliminated. Total costs (line E) are the sum of fixed costs (line F) and variable costs. Variable costs are represented by line

    A. A B. B C. C D. D

ROAD REPAIR COSTS IF PERFORMED BY CITY STAFF OR AN OUTSIDE CONTRACTOR

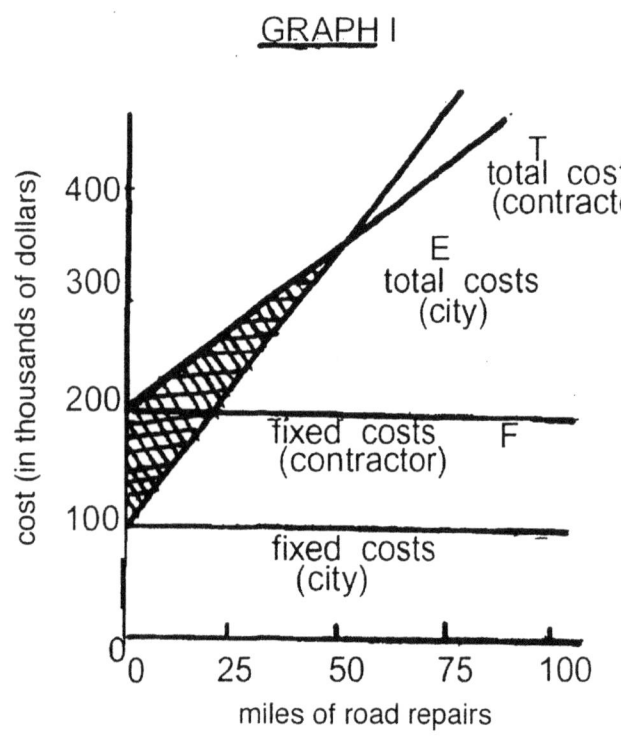
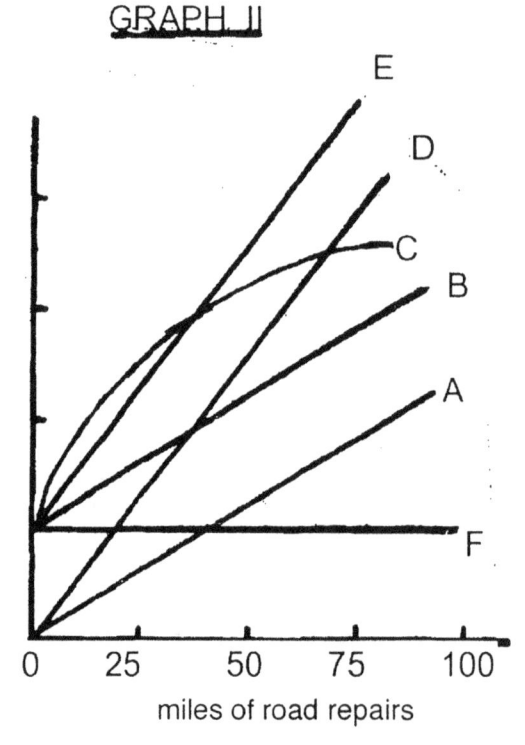

20. Fiscal experts in municipal affairs have contended that the most acute problem facing the city today seems to be the growth of the city's short-term debt.
Of the following, the LEAST likely reason for the city to engage in short-term borrowing is that the city

    A. expects money from long-term borrowing that it plans to undertake
    B. needs to be tided over until funds due from the Federal or State government arrive
    C. needs money to finance big construction outlays
    D. anticipates money from future tax collections

20.____

21. A MAJOR criticism of the *superagency* has been the

    A. additional layers of control and additional lines of command
    B. merger of departmental functions
    C. political manipulation
    D. professional incompetence in administration

21.____

22. The management of a large urban city is different in many ways from the management of other systems, particularly large business organizations.
The one of the following which does NOT exemplify these differences is:

    A. A mayor, in contrast to a manager of a large business, is often held responsible for services, etc., over which he has little authority.
    B. Top management of a large urban city must deal with a greater number of different pressures from diverse interest groups.
    C. The city government, in contrast to a large business organization, often lacks adequate management controls, and goals are often ill-defined.
    D. The multiplicity of alternatives available to city government as opposed to large businesses, are substantially greater, making decision-making haphazard.

22.____

23. The function called internal control applies to those measures taken by a government agency to protect its assets. Internal control has a role to play as an enforcer of administrative edicts as well as for purposes of asset protection.
Of the following statements relating to internal control, as described above, select the *one* usually considered to be LEAST valid.

    A. Internal control makes auditing by an external agency more difficult.
    B. The function of internal control often involves the auditing process.
    C. That people cannot be trusted to act wisely and honestly seems to be implicit in all the principles of internal control.
    D. Internal control is simply a form of self-audit by the agency itself.

23.____

24. In addition to the new effect on workers who are unskilled and undereducated, the severe effect of the high unemployment rate in the city has recently become MOST apparent among

    A. skilled craftsmen in the building trades
    B. clerical employees
    C. middle management personnel
    D. architects and engineers

24.____

25. The fact that the city has the second highest jobless rate of any major U.S. city except Detroit is considered particularly significant because, compared to Detroit, unemployment in the city   25.____

    A. is caused by city government fiscal measures rather than private business conditions
    B. exists in more than one industry
    C. results in an increase in welfare expenditures to a greater extent
    D. more seriously affects the world-wide economy

KEY (CORRECT ANSWERS)

1. D		11. D	
2. D		12. D	
3. A		13. A	
4. A		14. A	
5. C		15. B	
6. A		16. B	
7. D		17. C	
8. A		18. A	
9. C		19. D	
10. A		20. C	

21. A
22. D
23. A
24. A
25. B

EXAMINATION SECTION
TEST 1

DIRECTIONS: Each question or incomplete statement is followed by several suggested answers or completions. Select the one that BEST answers the question or completes the statement. *PRINT THE LETTER OF THE CORRECT ANSWER IN THE SPACE AT THE RIGHT.*

1. The MOST important factor in establishing a disciplinary policy in an organization is

    A. consistency of application
    B. strict supervisors
    C. strong enforcement
    D. the degree of toughness or laxity

2. The FIRST step in planning a program is to

    A. clearly define the objectives
    B. estimate the costs
    C. hire a program director
    D. solicit funds

3. The PRIMARY purpose of control in an organization is to

    A. punish those who do not do their job well
    B. get people to do what is necessary to achieve an objective
    C. develop clearly stated rules and regulations
    D. regulate expenditures

4. After a procedures manual has been written and distributed,

    A. continuous maintenance work is necessary to keep the manual current
    B. it is best to issue new manuals rather than make changes in the original manual
    C. no changes should be necessary
    D. only major changes should be considered

5. Of the following, the MOST important criterion of effective report writing is

    A. eloquence of writing style
    B. the use of technical language
    C. to be brief and to the point
    D. to cover all details

6. The use of electronic data processing

    A. has proven unsuccessful in most organizations
    B. has unquestionable advantages for all organizations
    C. is unnecessary in most organizations
    D. should be decided upon only after careful feasibility studies by individual organizations

7. Of the following methods, which would normally be MOST appropriate to validate a new aptitude test?

    A. Concurrent
    B. Construct
    C. Content
    D. Predictive

8. The PRIMARY purpose of work measurement is to

   A. design and install a wage incentive program
   B. determine who should be promoted
   C. establish a yardstick to determine extent of progress
   D. set up a spirit of competition among employees

9. A hypothetical construct is BEST defined as an(any)

   A. speculation that a researcher wishes to articulate
   B. entity or process presumed to exist but currently unable to be observed
   C. explanation of what antecedent conditions lead to various consequences
   D. expression of the relationship between stimulus and response variables

10. Representative samples are

    A. always drawn from finite populations
    B. always drawn from infinite populations
    C. drawn in a random, unbiased manner and have the characteristics of the larger universe
    D. larger than stratified samples

11. Interval or equal-interval scales have

    A. an absolute or natural zero that has empirical meaning
    B. none of the characteristics of nominal and ordinal scales
    C. no validity
    D. the property that numerically equal distances on the scale represent equal distances in the property being measured

12. Protective techniques of obtaining and analyzing information from respondents are

    A. designed so that subjects will respond as frankly as possible
    B. easier to analyze than objective techniques
    C. forms of structured scales
    D. to be avoided at all costs

13. Of the following, which is NOT a descriptive research design? _____ study.

    A. Case
    B. Correlation
    C. Developmental
    D. Pretest-posttest

14. One method of testing hypotheses using available materials produced by institutions, organizations, and individuals is

    A. content analysis
    B. distance-cluster analysis
    C. semantic differential
    D. sociometric analysis

15. The MOST important difference between experimental research and ex post facto research is

    A. analysis of data required
    B. control of the variables
    C. cost of the study
    D. length of time required to conduct the study

16. *The public health department of a large city wishes to study the effect of different chemicals on the retardation of tooth decay in children. Three groups of children ranging in age from 10 to 15 are selected randomly. One group of children is given toothpaste containing chemical X and another group is given toothpaste with chemical Y. A third group is given toothpaste with no chemical added. All three groups are given the same kind of toothbrush and are asked to brush their teeth twice a day for one year using the toothpaste and toothbrushes they have received. Periodic dental check-ups are made of the children in all three groups to determine the amount of tooth decay.*
    In the above study, the independent and dependent variables may BEST be defined as follows:

    A. chemicals X and Y and toothbrushes are independent variables and the amount of tooth decay is the dependent variable
    B. chemicals X and Y are independent variables and the amount of tooth decay is the dependent variable
    C. chemicals X and Y, toothbrushes, and the number of times a day the children brush their teeth are dependent variables and the amount of tooth decay is the independent variable
    D. chemicals X and Y, toothbrushes, and the number of times a day the children brush their teeth are independent variables and the amount of tooth decay is the dependent variable

17. A research hypothesis may BEST be defined as a(n)

    A. problem statement concerning two or more unknown variables
    B. speculation based on the researcher"s experience
    C. statement of expectation concerning the relations between variables which can be tested
    D. expository statement of the statistical procedure to be used in the research

18. A review of the literature is included in the research report PRIMARILY in order to

    A. demonstrate the scope of the investigator's knowledge about the research problem
    B. develop the theoretical foundation of the study
    C. indicate the literature reviewed by the investigator in planning the study
    D. save the reader time

19. The null hypothesis is a statistical proposition which states that

    A. no explanation of differences between variables should be accepted completely
    B. no differences exist between two or more sample means
    C. no variable can be accurately measured
    D. the real difference between the variables of the problem is greater than one would expect by chance

20. The following scores were obtained by an elementary mathematics class at the end of one year of instruction:

    | 11 | 19 | 17 |
    | 2 | 15 | 6 |
    | 5 | 6 | 8 |

    If the score of 8 were changed to 10, the mean(,)
    A. and median of this group of data would change but the mode would remain the same
    B. median, and mode would change
    C. median, and mode would remain the same
    D. of this group of data would change but the median would remain the same

    20.____

21. The normal distribution which is represented by a theoretical bell-shaped curve has the following property:

    A. Exactly .6826 of the total area will fall between an ordinate of two standard deviations above the mean
    B. It is a fictional curve having no real function
    C. The mean and median will coincide and have exactly the same value
    D. The total area under the curve is equal to 2.98

    21.____

22. In the case of variables that are linearly related, the correlation coefficient is a measure of

    A. the causal relationship present between variables
    B. the difference between the mean and the standard deviation
    C. the direction and degree of the relationship between variables
    D. which variable is independent and which is dependent

    22.____

23. If a student's score on the final examination in a chemistry class is at the 72nd percentile, one can SAFELY assume that

    A. the student answered 7 more questions correctly than did a student whose score was at the 65th percentile
    B. 72% of the class scored lower than this student
    C. the student answered 72 out of 100 questions correctly
    D. the student is above average in chemistry

    23.____

24. The significance level of a statistic is the probability that

    A. a Type II error has been committed
    B. the obtained result of the statistic could occur by chance
    C. the outcome of the experiment is $\bar{X}_1 \neq \bar{X}_2$
    D. there is a positive relationship between the variables being measured

    24.____

25. The standard error of the mean is an estimate of

    A. how far the sample mean is likely to differ from the population mean
    B. how far two sample means differ from each other
    C. the amount of error committed in computation
    D. the amount of error inherent in the population mean

    25.____

26. Nonparametric statistics are different from parametric statistics in that   26.____

    A. conditions about the population parameters are not specified in nonparametric tests
    B. nonparametric statistics are easier and faster to compute
    C. the measures to be analyzed by nonparametric tests must be continuous
    D. the measures to be analyzed by parametric statistics must be discrete

27. The Chi square test CANNOT be used reliably when the   27.____

    A. population distribution is not assumed to be normal
    B. population distribution is positively skewed
    C. samples are very large
    D. samples are very small

28. Of the following, the MOST critical problem faced by metropolitan educational systems is   28.____

    A. inadequate physical facilities
    B. parental indifference
    C. the lack of motivation to learn among urban youth
    D. the rapidity and magnitude of population change

29. In reference to educational systems, the concept of community control   29.____

    A. advocates that parents should take the place of professional educators
    B. implies that all educational decisions should be voted upon in open community meetings
    C. is essentially the same as decentralization
    D. represents the idea that the ultimate authority to make policy decisions rests with community representatives

30. Of the following, the MOST serious drawback to the *grant-in-aid* approach to support community services is that   30.____

    A. grants are difficult to obtain
    B. it encourages overcentralization of services
    C. it has had little or no provision for coordination of services
    D. it is too expensive

31. Of the following, the BEST definition of records management is   31.____

    A. storage of all types of records at minimum expense
    B. planned control of all types of records
    C. storage of records for maximum accessibility
    D. systematic filing of all types of records

32. The title of a contemporary best-selling book by Robert Townsend is .   32.____

    A. MANAGEMENT ANALYSIS: WAVE OF THE FUTURE
    B. MANAGEMENT FOR RESULTS
    C. THE HUMAN SIDE OF ENTERPRISE
    D. UP THE ORGANIZATION

33. A summary punched card containing totals of a group of similar detail cards is GENERALLY called a _____ card.

    A. master unit record
    B. summary unit record
    C. total
    D. unit record

34. One of the more famous studies of organizations is called the Hawthorne study. This work was one of the first to point out the importance of

    A. employees' benefit and retirement programs
    B. informal organization among employees
    C. job engineering
    D. styles of position classification

35. In organization theory, the type of position in which an individual is appointed to give technical aid to management on a particular problem area is generally BEST termed a(n)

    A. administrative assistant
    B. *assistant to*
    C. staff assistant
    D. staff specialist

36. In analyzing data for the acquisition of new equipment, a methods analyst gathers the facts, analyzes them, and develops new procedures which will be required when the new equipment arrives.
    In analyzing the factors involved, which one of the following is normally LEAST important in the evaluation of new equipment?

    A. Cost factors
    B. Layout and installation factors
    C. Production planning
    D. Operational experience of manufacturers of allied equipment

37. The one of the following which is NOT a primary objective of a records retention and disposal system is to

    A. assure appropriate preservation of records having permanent value
    B. dispose of records not warranting further preservation
    C. establish retention standards for archives
    D. provide an opportunity to use miniaturization techniques to simplify filing systems

38. In organizing, doing what *works* in the particular situation, with due regard to both short and long range objectives, is BEST termed

    A. ambivalence
    B. authoritarianism
    C. decentralization
    D. pragmatism

39. If an effort were made to reduce the number of private offices in a new layout, the LEAST effective substitute in offering privacy would be the use of

    A. an open area, with lower movable partitions or railings separating each individual
    B. conference rooms
    C. larger desks
    D. modular desk units

40. The term *administrative substation* NORMALLY refers to   40._____
    A. a work station handling a number of office services for an office organization
    B. a work station where middle level supervisors are located
    C. an office for handling management trainees
    D. the functions allocated to particular levels of administrative managers

---

KEY (CORRECT ANSWERS)

1. A	11. D	21. C	31. B
2. A	12. A	22. C	32. D
3. B	13. D	23. B	33. B
4. A	14. A	24. B	34. B
5. C	15. B	25. A	35. D
6. D	16. B	26. A	36. D
7. D	17. C	27. D	37. D
8. C	18. B	28. D	38. D
9. B	19. B	29. D	39. C
10. C	20. A	30. C	40. A

TEST 2

DIRECTIONS: Each question or incomplete statement is followed by several suggested answers or completions. Select the one that BEST answers the question or completes the statement. *PRINT THE LETTER OF THE CORRECT ANSWER IN THE SPACE AT THE RIGHT.*

1. A research technique which would be applied to determine the optimum number of window clerks or interviewers to have in an agency serving the public would MOST likely be the use of

    A. line of balance
    B. queuing theory
    C. simulation
    D. work sampling

    1.____

2. A type of file which permits the operator to remain seated while the file can be moved backward and forward as required is BEST termed a ___ file.

    A. lateral
    B. movable
    C. reciprocating
    D. rotary

    2.____

3. The technique of work measurement in which the analyst observes the work at random times of the day is BEST termed

    A. indirect observation
    B. logging
    C. ratio delay
    D. wristwatch

    3.____

4. Examples of predetermined time systems generally should include all of the following EXCEPT

    A. Master Clerical Data
    B. Methods Time Measurement
    C. Short Interval Data
    D. Work Factor

    4.____

5. A technique by which the supervisor or an assistant distributes a predetermined batch of work to the employees at periodic intervals of the day is generally BEST known as

    A. backlog control scheduling
    B. production control scheduling
    C. short interval scheduling
    D. workload balancing

    5.____

6. Wright Bakke defined his *fusion process* as the

    A. work environment to some degree remakes the organization and the organization to some degree remakes the work environment
    B. fusing of the interests of both management and labor unions
    C. community of interest between first line supervisors and top management
    D. organization to some degree remakes the individual and the individual to some degree remakes the organization

    6.____

7. If a staff analyst is required to recommend the selection of a machine for an office operation, he can BEST judge the expected output of a particular machine by pursuing which of the following courses of action?
    Obtaining

    A. an actual test run of the machine in his office
    B. data from the manufacturer of the machine
    C. information on the percentage of working time the machine will be used
    D. the experience of actual users of similar machines elsewhere

    7.____

8. In planning office space for a newly established bureau, it would usually be LEAST desirable to

   A. concentrate, rather than disperse, the chief sources of office noises
   B. design an office environment with about the same brightness as the office desk
   C. designate as reception rooms, washrooms, and other service areas those areas that will receive lesser amounts of illumination than those areas in which private office work will be performed
   D. eliminate natural light in cases where it is not the major light source

9. A private office should be used when its use is dictated by facts and unbiased judgment. It should never be provided simply because requests and sometimes pressure have been brought to bear.
   Of the following reasons used to justify use of a private office, the one that requires the MOST care in determining whether a private office is actually warranted is

   A. an office has always been provided for a particular job
   B. prestige considerations
   C. the confidential nature of the work
   D. the work involves high concentration

10. Theoretically, an ideal organization structure can be set up for each enterprise. In actual practice, the ideal organization structure is seldom, if ever, obtained.
    Of the following, the one that normally is of LEAST influence in determining the organization structure is the

    A. existence of agreements and favors among members of the organization
    B. funds available
    C. opinions and beliefs of top executives
    D. tendency of management to discard established forms in favor of new forms

11. An IMPORTANT aspect to keep in mind during the decision-making process is that

    A. all possible alternatives for attaining goals should be sought out and considered
    B. considering various alternatives only leads to confusion
    C. once a decision has been made, it cannot be retracted
    D. there is only one correct method to reach any goal

12. Implementation of accountability requires

    A. a leader who will not hesitate to take punitive action
    B. an established system of communication from the bottom to the top
    C. explicit directives from leaders
    D. too much expense to justify it

13. Of the following, the MAJOR difference between systems and procedures analysis and work simplification is

    A. the former complicates organizational routine and the latter simplifies it
    B. the former is objective and the latter is subjective
    C. the former generally utilizes expert advice and the latter is a *do-it-yourself* improvement by supervisors and workers
    D. there is no difference other than in name

14. Systems development is concerned with providing

    A. a specific set of work procedures
    B. an overall framework to describe general relationships
    C. definitions of particular organizational functions
    D. organizational symbolism

15. Organizational systems and procedures should be

    A. developed as problems arise as no design can anticipate adequately the requirements of an organization
    B. developed jointly by experts in systems and procedures and the people who are responsible for implementing them
    C. developed solely by experts in systems and procedures
    D. eliminated whenever possible to save unnecessary expense

16. The CHIEF danger of a decentralized control system is that

    A. excessive reports and communications will be generated
    B. problem areas may not be detected readily
    C. the expense will become prohibitive
    D. this will result in too many *chiefs*

17. Of the following, management guides and controls clerical work PRINCIPALLY through

    A. close supervision and constant checking of personnel
    B. spot checking of clerical procedures
    C. strong sanctions for clerical supervisors
    D. the use of printed forms

18. Which of the following is MOST important before conducting fact-finding interviews?

    A. Becoming acquainted with all personnel to be interviewed
    B. Explaining the techniques you plan to use
    C. Explaining to the operating officials the purpose and scope of the study
    D. Orientation of the physical layout

19. Of the following, the one that is NOT essential in carrying out a comprehensive work improvement program is

    A. standards of performance
    B. supervisory training
    C. work count/task list
    D. work distribution chart

20. Which of the following control techniques is MOST useful on large, complex systems projects?

    A. A general work plan
    B. Gantt Chart
    C. Monthly progress report
    D. PERT Chart

21. The action which is MOST effective in gaining acceptance of a study by the agency which is being studied is

    A. a directive from the agency head to install a study based on recommendations included in a report
    B. a lecture-type presentation following approval of the procedures
    C. a written procedure in narrative form covering the proposed system with visual presentations and discussions
    D. procedural charts showing the *before* and *after* situation, forms, steps, etc. to the employees affected

22. Which of the following is NOT an advantage in the use of oral instructions as compared with written instructions? Oral instruction(s)

    A. can easily be changed
    B. is superior in transmitting complex directives
    C. facilitate exchange of information between a superior and his subordinate
    D. without discussions make it easier to ascertain understanding

23. Which organization principle is MOST closely related to procedural analysis and improvement?

    A. Duplication, overlapping, and conflict should be eliminated.
    B. Managerial authority should be clearly defined.
    C. The objectives of the organization should be clearly defined.
    D. Top management should be freed of burdensome detail.

24. Which of the following is the MAJOR objective of operational audits?

    A. Detecting fraud
    B. Determining organization problems
    C. Determining the number of personnel needed
    D. Recommending opportunities for improving operating and management practices

25. Of the following, the formalization of organization structure is BEST achieved by

    A. a narrative description of the plan of organization
    B. functional charts
    C. job descriptions together with organization charts
    D. multi-flow charts

26. Budget planning is MOST useful when it achieves

    A. cost control
    B. forecast of receipts
    C. performance review
    D. personnel reduction

27. The underlying principle of sound administration is to

    A. base administration on investigation of facts
    B. have plenty of resources available
    C. hire a strong administrator
    D. establish a broad policy

28. Although questionnaires are not the best survey tool the management analyst has to use, there are times when a good questionnaire can expedite the *fact-finding* phase of a management survey.
Which of the following should be AVOIDED in the design and distribution of the questionnaire?

   A. Questions should be framed so that answers can be classified and tabulated for analysis.
   B. Those receiving the questionnaire must be knowledgeable enough to accurately provide the information desired.
   C. The questionnaire should enable the respondent to answer in a narrative manner.
   D. The questionnaire should require a minimum amount of writing.

29. Of the following, the formula which is used to calculate the arithmetic mean from data grouped in a frequency distribution is

   A. $M = \dfrac{N}{\Sigma fX}$
   B. $M = N(\Sigma fX)$
   C. $M = \dfrac{\Sigma fX}{N}$
   D. $M = \dfrac{\Sigma X}{fN}$

30. Arranging large groups of numbers in frequency distributions

   A. gives a more composite picture of the total group than a random listing
   B. is misleading in most cases
   C. is unnecessary in most instances
   D. presents the data in a form whereby further manipulation of the group is eliminated

31. After a budget has been developed, it serves to

   A. assist the accounting department in posting expenditures
   B. measure the effectiveness of department managers
   C. provide a yardstick against which actual costs are measured
   D. provide the operating department with total expenditures to date

32. Of the following, which formula is used to determine staffing requirements?

   A. $\dfrac{\text{Hours per man-day}}{\text{Volume X Standard}} = \text{Employees Needed}$
   B. $\dfrac{\text{Hours per man-day X Standard}}{\text{Volume}} = \text{Employees Needed}$
   C. $\dfrac{\text{Hours per man-day X Volume}}{\text{Standard}} = \text{Employees Needed}$
   D. $\dfrac{\text{Volume X Standard}}{\text{Hours per man-day}} = \text{Employees Needed}$

33. Of the following, which formula is used to determine the number of days required to process work?

A. $\dfrac{\text{Employees} \times \text{Daily Output}}{\text{Volume}}$ = Days to Process Work

B. $\dfrac{\text{Employees} \times \text{Volume}}{\text{Daily Output}}$ = Days to Process Work

C. $\dfrac{\text{Volume}}{\text{Employees} \times \text{Daily Output}}$ = Days to Process Work

D. $\dfrac{\text{Volume} \times \text{Daily Output}}{\text{Employees}}$ = Days to Process Work

34. Identify this symbol, as used in a Systems Flow Chart.
    A. Document
    B. Decision
    C. Preparation
    D. Process

35. Of the following, the MAIN advantage of a form letter over a dictated letter is that a form letter
    A. is more expressive
    B. is neater
    C. may be mailed in a window envelope
    D. requires less secretarial time

36. The term that may be defined as a systematic analysis of all factors affecting work being done or all factors that will affect work to be done, in order to save effort, time or money is
    A. flow process charting
    B. work flow analysis
    C. work measurement
    D. work simplification

37. Generally, the LEAST important basic factor to be considered in developing office layout improvements is to locate
    A. office equipment, reference facilities, and files as close as practicable to those using them
    B. persons as close as practicable to the persons from whom they receive their work
    C. persons as close as practicable to windows and/or adequate ventilation
    D. persons who are friendly with each other close together to improve morale

38. Of the following, the one which is LEAST effective in reducing administrative costs is
    A. applying objective measurement techniques to determine the time required to perform a given task
    B. establishing budgets on the basis of historical performance data
    C. motivating supervisors and managers in the importance of cost reduction
    D. selecting the best method - manual, mechanical, or electronic - to process the essential work

39. *Fire-fighting* is a common expression in management terminology. Of the following, which BEST describes *fire-fighting* as an analyst's approach to solving paperwork problems?

    A. A complete review of all phases of the department's processing functions
    B. A studied determination of the proper equipment to process the work
    C. An analysis of each form that is being processed and the logical reasons for its processing
    D. The solution of problems as they arise, usually at the request of operating personnel

39.____

40. Assume that an analyst with a proven record of accomplishment on many projects is having difficulties on his present assignment.
    Of the following, the BEST course of action for his superior to take is to

    A. assume there is a personality conflict involved and transfer the analyst to another project
    B. give the analyst some time off
    C. review the nature of the project to determine whether or not the analyst is equipped to handle the assignment
    D. suggest that the analyst seek counseling

40.____

KEY (CORRECT ANSWERS)

1.	B	11.	A	21.	C	31.	C
2.	C	12.	B	22.	B	32.	D
3.	C	13.	C	23.	A	33.	C
4.	C	14.	B	24.	D	34.	A
5.	C	15.	B	25.	C	35.	D
6.	D	16.	B	26.	A	36.	D
7.	A	17.	D	27.	A	37.	D
8.	D	18.	C	28.	C	38.	B
9.	A	19.	B	29.	C	39.	D
10.	D	20.	D	30.	A	40.	C

EXAMINATION SECTION
TEST 1

DIRECTIONS: Each question or incomplete statement is followed by several suggested answers or completions. Select the one that BEST answers the question or completes the statement. *PRINT THE LETTER OF THE CORRECT ANSWER IN THE SPACE AT THE RIGHT.*

1. The number of figures to be retained in the sum of squares to the right of the decimal place in an analysis of variance problems can BEST be determined by making an estimate of the
   A. total number of degrees of freedom
   B. coefficient of variation
   C. standard error of measurement
   D. homogeneity of treatment variances
   E. regression equation

2. The experimental design that requires the LEAST number of subjects to test an hypothesis involving three methods of teaching, three intelligence levels, and three varieties of subject matter is the
   A. factorial design
   B. Latin square design
   C. random replications design
   D. Graeco-Latin square design
   E. split-half technique

3. Factorial designs, such as the Latin or Graeco-Latin squares, have as their PRIMARY objective the estimation of the effects of
   A. the interaction of control and experimental groups
   B. a control variable
   C. covariance on the independent variable
   D. several variables
   E. confidence intervals

4. Suppose a research worker is studying the differential incidence of poliomyelitis among school children in the several districts of a large city. The sampling distribution which will be MOST likely to fit his data is the
   A. chi square
   B. normal
   C. Poisson
   D. binomial
   E. rank-difference method

5. The method MOST recently advocated by psychologists for handling the profile-similarity problem is _____ analysis.
   A. multivariate
   B. factor
   C. canonical correlation
   D. multiple correlation
   E. interaction

6. Which pair of parameters is an experimenter required to estimate in order to specify the mathematical form of a normal distribution of scores in the population?
   Mean and standard
   A. error of measurement
   B. error of estimate
   C. ordinate
   D. deviation
   E. score

7. Which of the following processes fails to satisfy the criterion of randomness in the selection of an approximately 16 percent sample of experimental subjects from a population?
   A. Assignment of a sequence of integers to the elements of the population and the subsequent use of a randomly entered table of random numbers to select 16 percent of the supply
   B. Alphabetical arrangement of the subjects' names and the selection of every sixth name for the sample
   C. Rolling one of a pair of dice once for each element in the population and selection of those elements for which a "six" was obtained
   D. Use of a "draft-type" lottery system in which the name of every subject in the population is placed in an identical capsule and the capsules are drawn singly from a bowl with a thorough mixing between draws.
   E. None of the above

8. The CORRECT use of the biserial correlation coefficient as an estimate of "rho" involves the following assumption:
   A. One of the variables is continuously and normally distributed and the other is a true dichotomy.
   B. Both the underlying variables are continuously and normally distributed.
   C. The sampling distribution of biserial "r" is known and is independent of the nature of the distributions of the variables.
   D. Both variables are true dichotomies, hence they represent discrete data.
   E. Both variables tend to be spuriously high in the standard group.

9. The PRIMARY purpose of replication as a principle of experimental design is to
   A. control outside variables which would provide alternative explanations of the results
   B. supply an estimate of error by which to judge the significance of certain comparisons
   C. increase the precision of the experiment
   D. make the test material more homogeneous than it would otherwise be
   E. decrease the precision of the experiment

10. Of which of the following statistics is the sampling distribution somewhat asymmetrical?
    A. Biased estimate of the variance
    B. Difference between two means
    C. Product moment correlation coefficient where the parameter is zero
    D. Unbiased estimate of the variance
    E. None of the above

11. An economical correlation index which approximates the biserial "r" under certain sampling conditions in item selection was developed by
    A. Guilford
    B. Thompson
    C. Flanagan
    D. Student
    E. Fisher

12. Read each statement.
    Statement I: In the interpretation of the results of factorial experiments, factors which produce large main effects tend to have significant interactions.
    Statement II: In the interpretation of the results of factorial experiments, factors which produce small main effects usually show few significant interactions.
    Then select:
    A. If I is true, but II is false
    B. If both I and II are true
    C. If II is true, but I is false
    D. If both I and II are false

13. Read each statement.
    Statement I: One assumption underlying the use of the analysis of variance is that the varieties are independently distributed in the normal distribution.
    Statement II: One assumption underlying the use of the analysis of variance is that the experimental errors are independently distributed in the normal distribution.
    Then select:
    A. If II is true, but I is false
    B. If both I and II are true
    C. If I is true, but II is false
    D. If both I and II are false

14. Read each statement.
    Statement I: The analysis of covariance can be used to isolate extraneous sources of variation in the experiment which are too costly or impractical to control as a separate factor.
    Statement II: The analysis of covariance can be used to increase the precision of an experiment.
    Then select:
    A. If both I and II are false
    B. If I is true, but II is false
    C. If II is true, but I is false
    D. If both I and II are true

Questions 15-17.

DIRECTIONS: Questions 15 through 17 are to be answered on the basis of the following table.

Abridged F-Table 1% Level
n_1 degrees of freedom for greater mean square

n_2	1....	2....	5....	10....	50....	∞
1	4052	4999	5764	6056	6302	6366
5	16.26	13.27	10.97	10.05	9.24	9.02
10	10.04	7.56	5.64	4.85	4.12	3.91
50	7.17	5.06	3.41	2.70	1.94	1.68
∞	6.64	4.60	3.02	2.32	1.52	1.00

15. Suppose you made a t-test of the difference between the test score means of two groups of students in which 50 degrees of freedom were available for testing significance. How could you use the above table to evaluate your results at the 1% significance level?
Compare the obtained t value with
   A. 6302
   B. the square root of 7.17
   C. the square root of 1.68
   D. 1.94
   E. 2.32

16. Suppose you wish to test the equality of test score variances for two separate samples of 51 students each. Under what condition would it be possible to obtain an F-value of 0.50 or less?
   A. The variance of one sample is twice that of the other.
   B. The degrees of freedom for one sample is 25 and the other is 50.
   C. The variance of one sample is half that of the other.
   D. The observed variance ratio is half that for infinity.
   E. It would be impossible to obtain such a value.

17. In a study of the Minnesota Teacher Attitude Inventory scores of three groups of undergraduates, Rabinowitz presented the following analysis of variance table:

Source	Degrees of Freedom	Sum of Squares	Mean Square
Between groups	2	344.39	172.19
Within groups	53	33342.11	629.10
Total	55	33686.50	

On the basis of this table and a pre-selected 1% significance level, he should
   A. reject the hypothesis of equal means with an F value of less than unity
   B. accept the hypothesis of equal means with an F value of 3.65
   C. accept the hypothesis of equal means with an F value less than unity
   D. reject the hypothesis of equal means with an F value of 3.65
   E. reject all of the above

18. A device, used in factorial designs, which eliminates the necessity of including every combination of treatments in each block is called
    A. confounding
    B. inter-block control
    C. replication
    D. randomization
    E. rational equivalence

19. The process of breaking up the total sum of squares of deviations of the observations from a grand mean into independent portions assigned to certain factors is called
    A. factor analysis
    B. the correlation ratio
    C. analysis of variance
    D. multi-variate analysis
    E. partial correlation

20. Of the following, the MOST appropriate method for obtaining the average intercorrelation among the rankings of five judges is
    A. Kendall's coefficient of concordance
    B. Hotelling's canonical correlation
    C. Fisher's discriminant function
    D. Spearman's rank correlation
    E. Wherry-Doolittle's test selection method

21. In the investigation of the effects of heredity and environment, twin studies such as those conducted at the University of Chicago usually represent an experimental attempt to
    A. control the environment and the heredity simultaneously
    B. control heredity and study the influence of different natural environments
    C. vary the environment and control heredity
    D. control the environment and study hereditary differences
    E. disregard both heredity and environment

22. The research by Davis and Havighurst suggesting genuine cultural differences in the socialization of middle class children as compared with lower class children was based upon
    A. individual attitude tests of parents
    B. guided interviews with mothers
    C. guided interviews with children
    D. guided observations of child-rearing
    E. guided interviews with teachers

23. Research evidence indicates that institutionalized children, who have been denied warmth of attention, affection, and stimulation, tend to lack the
    A. democratic understanding of conformity
    B. aggression required for leadership
    C. ability to relate adequately to and with adults
    D. hostility necessary to independence
    E. independence of attitude of normally-reared children

24. The CHIEF finding of Malle's study contrasting the relative effects of self-motivation and group-motivation was that
    A. self-motivation was consistently more efficient than group-motivation
    B. neither group-motivation nor self-motivation was consistently the most efficient
    C. group-motivation was consistently more efficient than self-motivation
    D. group-motivation situations were consistently preferred by the American school children in the study
    E. self-motivation had little or no effect upon group-motivation

25. Studies on retention of final examination material indicate that the proportion forgotten after three months to three years is about
    A. 5-15%
    B. 20-35%
    C. 40-80%
    D. 85-95%
    E. equal to that remembered

KEY (CORRECT ANSWERS)

1.	B		11.	C
2.	B		12.	B
3.	D		13.	A
4.	C		14.	D
5.	E		15.	B
6.	D		16.	E
7.	B		17.	C
8.	B		18.	A
9.	B		19.	C
10.	A		20.	A

21. B
22. B
23. C
24. A
25. C

TEST 2

DIRECTIONS: Each question or incomplete statement is followed by several suggested answers or completions. Select the one that BEST answers the question or completes the statement. *PRINT THE LETTER OF THE CORRECT ANSWER IN THE SPACE AT THE RIGHT.*

1. The dictum "positive traits are positively correlated" is generally borne out in studies of the relationship between mental ability and general school achievement. The TYPICAL correlation found is about
   A. .15   B. .30   C. .50   D. .85   E. .95

2. Experience with mental and apparatus tests for the prediction of success in specialized military occupations during the last war has suggested that general learning ability tests such as the AGCT are
   A. equally as effective as weighted combinations of specialized tests
   B. less effective than weighted combinations of specialized tests only
   C. more effective than weighted combinations of specialized tests only for carefully screened samples of applicants
   D. more effective than weighted combinations of specialized tests
   E. less reliable than weighted combinations of specialized tests only

3. As shown by the most recent investigations, the TOTAL vocabulary of the average first-grade child is approximately _____ words.
   A. 400   B. 800   C. 1600   D. 1800   E. 2000

4. In studying the influence of social attitudes on learning, Edwards found that people select and retain from a speech those items which
   A. are unrelated to their attitudes
   B. conflict with their attitudes
   C. fit their attitudes
   D. are inconsistent within the speech, regardless of their own particular attitudes
   E. are of general interest

5. In studies contrasting socio-economic backgrounds of leaders and non-leaders, the evidence indicates that leaders tend to be
   A. from superior socio-economic backgrounds
   B. equally from all castes and classes in the community
   C. predominantly from the upward-mobile lower-middle class
   D. predominantly from aristocratic families
   E. predominantly from the "school of hard knocks"

6. R.A. Fisher developed the mathematical model known as the "z-distribution". The quantity "z" is equal to _____ estimates of the same population variance.
   A. one-half the difference of the natural logarithms of two independent
   B. one-half the difference of the common logarithms of two dependent
   C. one-half the difference of the common logarithms of two independent
   D. one-half the difference of the natural logarithms of two dependent
   E. twice the difference of the natural logarithms of two independent

6._____

7. For objective selection of "minimum" vocabulary for the teaching of Spanish, the BEST resource is
   A. Thorndike and Lorge's semantic count
   B. Ogden Richards' Basic Spanish
   C. Burgess' vocabulary control list
   D. Keniston's Basic List of Spanish Words
   E. Doren's Diagnostic Reading Test

7._____

8. Of the following authors, who was MOST closely associated with the evaluation of student-growth in non-academic areas?
   A. P.J. Rulon   B. T.L. Kelley   C. L.L. Thurstone
   D. G.D. Spache   E. R.W. Tyler

8._____

9. Within the community public relations program, the groups MOST likely to be of maximum benefit to the public schools are _____ groups.
   A. political   B. industrial   C. medical
   D. civic service   E. taxpayers

9._____

Questions 10-11.

DIRECTIONS: Questions 10 and 11 are to be answered on the basis of the following.

There are occasions in research when we may justifiably rely on verbal or fairly general statements of fact. These occasions grow in part out of the nature of the material and in part out of the purposes for which one is doing research.

10. In the above statement, the author is referring to the
    A. need to justify various techniques of research
    B. role of qualitative data in research
    C. role of quantitative data in research
    D. need to justify various purposes of research
    E. role of approximation in research

10._____

11. According to the above statement, the author is implying that
    A. the ends define the means   B. the means define the ends
    C. purposes create facts   D. facts create purposes
    E. means and ends are related

11._____

12. Implied in the phrase "the whole is more than the sum of its parts" is the concept that
    A. one cannot sum parts separated from a whole
    B. the organization of parts is a dimension of the whole
    C. atomism is superior to holism
    D. the total is larger than a single part
    E. sometimes one cannot see the forests because of the trees

13. The employment of Yates' correction for continuity in the calculation of the chi-square statistic is useful when the
    A. expectations in the cells are small
    B. data are organized as three-way or four-way classifications
    C. number of cells is large
    D. number of cells is small
    E. expectations in the cells are large

14. The effect of repeating an identical group intelligence test with the same group of pupils is generally to obtain higher scores. This is known as the _____ effect.
    A. practice   B. spurious   C. contamination
    D. duplication   E. qualifying

15. The chief purposes of most tests of educational achievement is to rank examinees in the order of their attainments.
    This statement would NOT apply to which of the following tests?
    A. Standardized achievement test batteries
    B. Diagnostic tests
    C. Survey tests
    D. Skill tests
    E. Aptitude tests

16. If the overall estimated reliability coefficient of a test battery of five tests administered to a group of 9,000 high school pupils is .92, one may conclude that
    A. each test is reliable enough for use with any given high school class
    B. the test battery is reliable for all high school pupils
    C. each test in the battery is reliable enough for use with individual pupils
    D. confidence can be placed in the battery for use with pupils similar to the norm group
    E. the test battery is unreliable but valid

17. With which of the following organizations are SCAT and STEP associated?
    A. Educational Testing Service   B. Houghton Mifflin Company
    C. Psychological Corporation   D. World Book Company
    E. ACT

18. In studying the differences between two classes taught arithmetic by two different methods, an investigator found that the regressions of the control variable, intelligence, on the criterion variable, arithmetic achievement, were not homogeneous for the two classes.
Which of the following techniques would be MOST appropriate to employ in analyzing the data under these circumstances?
    A. Analysis of covariance technique
    B. Correlation ratio for the two classes separately
    C. Fisher's discriminant function technique
    D. Bartlett's test for homogeneity of variance
    E. Neyman Johnson technique

18.____

Questions 19-25.

DIRECTIONS: Questions 19 through 25 are to be answered on the basis of the following paragraphs. Indicate the correct answer. Select the answer
    A. if the paragraphs indicate it is true;
    B. if the paragraphs indicate it is probably true
    C. if the paragraphs indicate it is probably false
    D. if the paragraphs indicate it is false
    E. none of the above

The fallacy underlying what some might call the eighteenth and nineteenth century misconceptions of the nature of scientific investigations seems to lie in a mistaken analogy. Those who said they were investigating the structure of the universe imagined themselves as the equivalent of the early explorers and map makers. The explorers of the fifteenth and sixteenth centuries had opened up new worlds with the aid of imperfect maps; in their accounts of distant lands, there had been some false and some ambiguous statements. But by the time everyone came to believe the world was round, the maps of distant continents were beginning to assume a fairly consistent pattern. By the seventeenth century, methods of measuring space and time had laid the foundations for an accurate geography.

On this basic issue there is far from complete agreement among philosophers of science today. You can, each of you, choose your side and find highly distinguished advocates for the point of view you have selected. However, in view of the revolution in physics, anyone who now asserts that science is an exploration of the universe must be prepared to shoulder a heavy burden of proof. To my mind, the analogy between the map maker and the scientist is false. A scientific theory is not even the first approximation to a map; it is not a need; it is a policy – an economical and fruitful guide to action by scientific investigators.

19. The author thinks that 18th and 19th century science followed the same technique as the 15th century geographers.

19.____

20. The author disagrees with the philosophers who are labeled realists.

20.____

21. The author believes there is a permanent structure to the universe.

21.____

22. A scientific theory is an economical guide to exploring what cannot be known absolutely.

22.____

23. Philosphers of science accept the relativity implications of recent research   23.____
    in physics.

24. It is a matter of time and effort before modern scientists will be as successful   24.____
    as the geographers.

25. The author believes in an indeterminate universe.

KEY (CORRECT ANSWERS)

1.	C	11.	E
2.	B	12.	B
3.	E	13.	A
4.	C	14.	A
5.	A	15.	B
6.	A	16.	D
7.	D	17.	A
8.	E	18.	E
9.	D	19.	D
10.	B	20.	B

21. D
22. A
23. D
24. D
25. B

INTERPRETING STATISTICAL DATA
GRAPHS, CHARTS AND TABLES
EXAMINATION SECTION
TEST 1

DIRECTIONS: Each questioner incomplete statement is followed by several suggested answers or completions. Select the one that BEST answers the question or completes the statement. *PRINT THE LETTER OF THE CORRECT ANSWER IN THE SPACE AT THE RIGHT.*

Questions 1-3.

DIRECTIONS: Questions 1 through 3 are to be answered SOLELY on the basis of the following table.

QUARTERLY SALES REPORTED BY MAJOR INDUSTRY GROUPS

DECEMBER 2021 – FEBRUARY 2023
Reported Sales, Taxable & Non-Taxable (in Millions)

Industry Groups	12/21-2/22	3/22-5/22	6/22-8/22	9/22-11/22	12/22-2/23
Retailers	2,802	2,711	2,475	2,793	2,974
Wholesalers	2,404	2,237	2,269	2,485	2,974
Manufacturers	3,016	2,888	3,001	3,518	3,293
Services	1,034	1,065	984	1,132	1,092

1. The trend in total reported sales may be described as
    A. downward
    B. downward and upward
    C. horizontal
    D. upward

2. The two industry groups that reveal a similar seasonal pattern for the period December 2021 through November 2022 are
    A. retailers and manufacturers
    B. retailers and wholesalers
    C. wholesalers and manufacturers
    D. wholesalers and service

3. Reported sales were at a MINIMUM between
    A. December 2021 and February 2022
    B. March 2022 and May 2022
    C. June 2022 and August 2022
    D. September 2022 and November 2022

TEST 2

DIRECTIONS: Each question or incomplete statement is followed by several suggested answers or completions. Select the one that BEST answers the question or completes the statement. *PRINT THE LETTER OF THE CORRECT ANSWER IN THE SPACE AT THE RIGHT*

Questions 1-4.

DIRECTIONS: Questions 1 through 4 are to be answered SOLELY on the basis of the following information.

The income elasticity of demand for selected items of consumer demand in the United States are:

Item	Elasticity
Airline Travel	5.66
Alcohol	.62
Dentist Fees	1.00
Electric Utilities	3.00
Gasoline	1.29
Intercity Bus	1.89
Local Bus	1.41
Restaurant Meals	.75

1. The demand for the item listed below that would be MOST adversely affected by a decrease in income is

    A. alcohol
    B. electric utilities
    C. gasoline
    D. restaurant meals

2. The item whose relative change in demand would be the same as the relative change in income would be

    A. dentist fees
    B. gasoline
    C. restaurant meals
    D. none of the above

3. If income increases by 12 percent, the demand for restaurant meals may be expected to increase by

    A. 9 percent
    B. 12 percent
    C. 16 percent
    D. none of the above

4. On the basis of the above information, the item whose demand would be MOST adversely affected by an increase in the sales tax from 7 percent to 8 percent to be passed on to the consumer in the form of higher prices

    A. would be airline travel
    B. would be alcohol
    C. would be gasoline
    D. cannot be determined

TEST 3

DIRECTIONS: Each question or incomplete statement is followed by several suggested answers or completions. Select the one that BEST answers the question or completes the statement. *PRINT THE LETTER OF THE CORRECT ANSWER IN THE SPACE AT THE RIGHT.*

Questions 1-3.

DIRECTIONS: Questions 1 through 3 are to be answered SOLELY on the basis of the following graphs depicting various relationships in a single retail store.

GRAPH 1
RELATIONSHIP BETWEEN NUMBER OF CUSTOMERS STORE AND TIME OF DAY

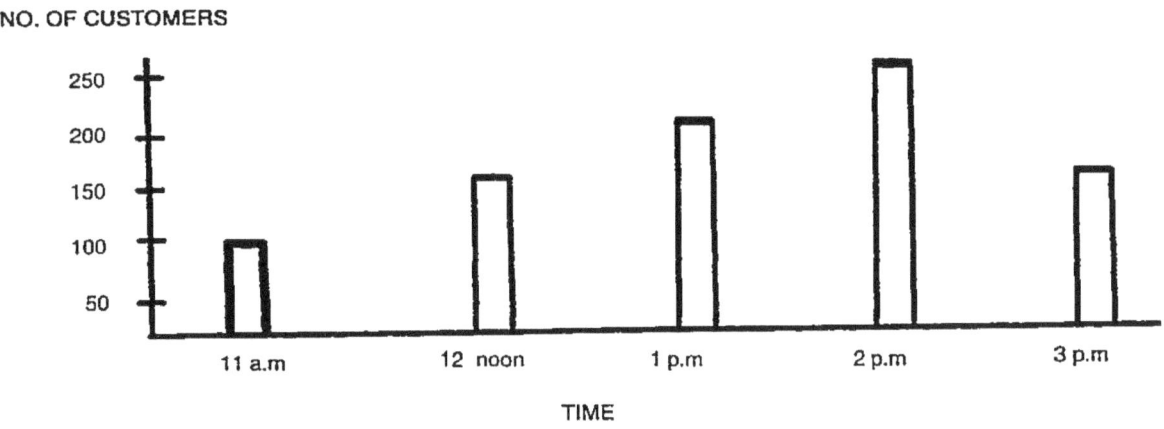

GRAPH II
RELATIONSHIP BETWEEN NUMBER OF CHECK-OUT LANES AVAILABLE IN STORE AND WAIT TIME FOR CHECK-OUT

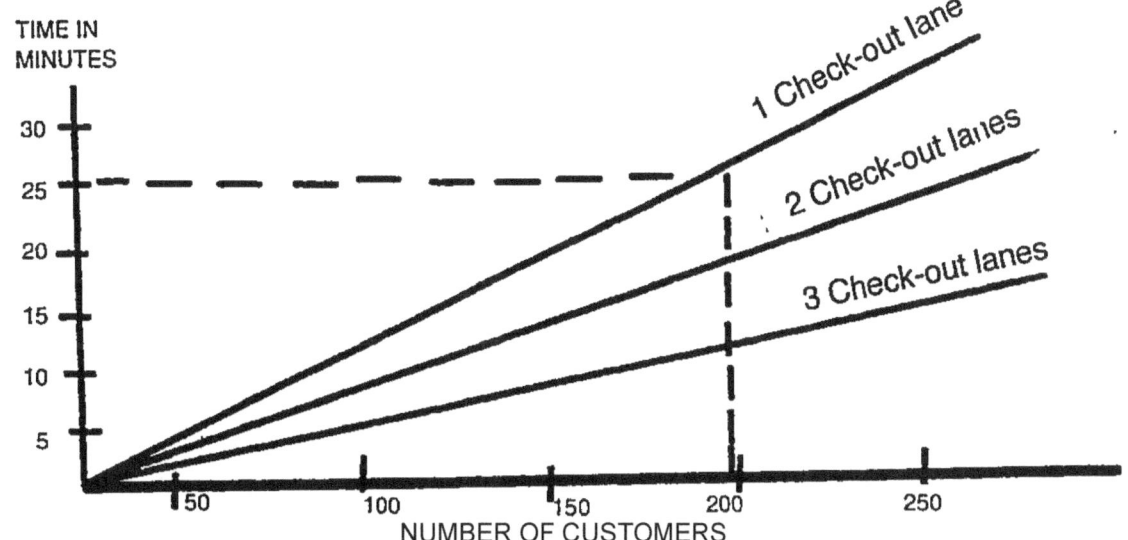

Note the dotted lines in Graph II. They demonstrate that, if there are 200 people in the store and only one check-out lane is open, the wait time will be 25 minutes.

1. At what time would a person be most likely NOT to have to wait more than 15 minutes if only one check-out lane is open?

    A. 11 A.M.   B. 12 Noon   C. 1 P.M.   D. 3 P.M.

2. At what time of day would a person have to wait the LONGEST to check out if three check-out lanes are available?

    A. 11 A.M.   B. 12 Noon   C. 1 P.M.   D. 2 P.M

3. The difference in wait times between 1 and 3 check-out lanes at 3 P.M. is MOST NEARLY

    A. 5   B. 10   C. 15   D. 20

TEST 4

DIRECTIONS: Each question or incomplete statement is followed by several suggested answers or completions. Select the one that BEST answers the question or completes the statement. *PRINT THE LETTER OF THE CORRECT ANSWER IN THE SPACE AT THE RIGHT.*

Questions 1-4.

DIRECTIONS: Questions 1 through 4 are to be answered SOLELY on the basis of the graph below.

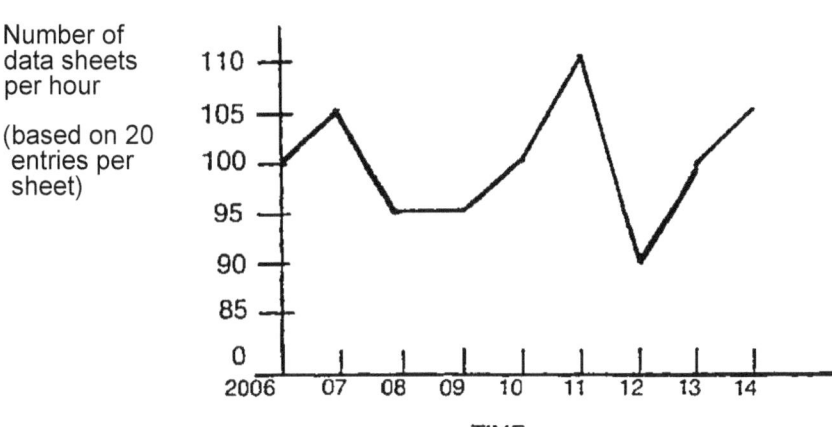

1. Of the following, during what four-year period did the average output of computer operators fall BELOW 100 sheets per hour?

    A. 2007-10   B. 2008-11   C. 2010-13   D. 2011-14

2. The average percentage change in output over the previous year's output for the years 2009 to 2012 is MOST NEARLY

    A. 2   B. 0   C. -5   D. -7

3. The difference between the actual output for 2012 and the projected figure based upon the average increase from 2006-2011 is MOST NEARLY

    A. 18   B. 20   C. 22   D. 24

4. Assume that after constructing the above graph you, an analyst, discovered that the average number of entries per sheet in 2012 was 25 (instead of 20) because of the complex nature of the work performed during that period.
The average output in sheets per hour for the period 2010-13, expressed in terms of 20 items per sheet, would then be MOST NEARLY

    A. 95   B. 100   C. 105   D. 110

63

TEST 6

DIRECTIONS: Each question or incomplete statement is followed by several suggested answers or completions. Select the one that BEST answers the question or completes the statement. *PRINT THE LETTER OF THE CORRECT ANSWER IN THE SPACE AT THE RIGHT.*

Questions 1-3.

DIRECTIONS: Questions 1 through 3 are to be answered on the basis of the following data assembled for a cost-benefit analysis.

	Cost	Benefit
No program	0	0
Alternative W	$ 3,000	$ 6,000
Alternative X	$10,000	$17,000
Alternative Y	$17,000	$25,000
Alternative Z	$30,000	$32,000

1. From the point of view of selecting the alternative with the best cost benefit ratio, the BEST alternative is Alternative

   A. W B. X C. Y D. Z

2. From the point of view of selecting the alternative with the best measure of net benefit, the BEST alternative is Alternative

   A. W B. X C. Y D. Z

3. From the point of view of pushing public expenditure to the point where marginal benefit equals or exceeds marginal cost, the BEST alternative is Alternative

   A. W B. X C. Y D. Z

TEST 6

DIRECTIONS: Each question or incomplete statement is followed by several suggested answers or completions. Select the one that BEST answers the question or completes the statement. *PRINT THE LETTER OF THE CORRECT ANSWER IN THE SPACE AT THE RIGHT.*

Questions 1-3.

DIRECTIONS: Questions 1 through 3 are to be answered SOLELY on the basis of the following data.

A series of cost-benefit studies of various alternative health programs yields the following results:

Program	Benefit	Cost
K	30	15
L	60	60
M	300	150
N	600	500

In answering Questions 1 and 2, assume that all programs can be increased or decreased in scale without affecting their individual benefit-to-cost ratios.

1. The benefit-to-cost ratio of Program M is

   A. 10:1   B. 5:1   C. 2:1   D. 1:2

2. The budget ceiling for one or more of the programs included in the study is set at 75 units. It may MOST logically be concluded that

   A. Programs K and L should be chosen to fit within the budget ceiling
   B. Program K would be the most desirable one that could be afforded
   C. Program M should be chosen rather than Program K
   D. the choice should be between Programs M and K

3. If no assumptions can be made regarding the effects of change of scale, the MOST logical conclusion, on the basis of the data available, is that

   A. more data are needed for a budget choice of program
   B. Program K is the most preferable because of its low cost and good benefit-to-cost ratio
   C. Program M is the most preferable because of its high benefits and good benefit-to-cost ratio
   D. there is no difference between Programs K and M, and either can be chosen for any purpose

TEST 7

DIRECTIONS: Each question or incomplete statement is followed by several suggested answers or completions. Select the one that BEST answers the question or completes the statement. *PRINT THE LETTER OF THE CORRECT ANSWER IN THE SPACE AT THE RIGHT.*

Questions 1-6.

DIRECTIONS: Questions 1 through 6 are to be answered SOLELY on the basis of the information contained in the charts below which relate to the budget allocations of City X, a small suburban community. The charts depict the annual budget allocations by Department and by expenditures over a five-year period.

CITY X BUDGET IN MILLIONS OF DOLLARS
TABLE I. Budget Allocations by Department

Department	2017	2018	2019	2020	2021
Public Safety	30	45	50	40	50
Health and Welfare	50	75	90	60	70
Engineering	5	8	10	5	8
Human Resources	10	12	20	10	22
Conservation & Environment	10	15	20	20	15
Education & Development	15	25	35	15	15
TOTAL BUDGET	120	180	225	150	180

TABLE II. Budget Allocations by Expenditures

Category	2017	2018	2019	2020	2021
Raw Materials & Machinery	36	63	68	30	98
Capital Outlay	12	27	56	15	18
Personal Services	72	90	101	105	64
TOTAL BUDGET	120	180	225	150	180

1. The year in which the SMALLEST percentage of the total annual budget was allocated to the Department of Education and Development is

   A. 2017 B. 2018 C. 2020 D. 2021

2. Assume that in 2020 the Department of Conservation and Environment divided its annual budget into the three categories of expenditures and in exactly the same proportion as the budget shown in Table II for the year 2020. The amount allocated for capital outlay in the Department of Conservation and Environment's 2020 budget was MOST NEARLY _____ million.

   A. $2 B. $4 C. $6 D. $10

2 (#9)

3. From the year 2018 to the year 2020, the sum of the annual budgets for the Departments of Public Safety and Engineering showed an overall _____ million.

    A. decline; S8
    C. decline; S15
    B. increase; $7
    D. increase; S22

4. The LARGEST dollar increase in departmental budget allocations from one year to the next was in _____ from _____.

    A. Public Safety; 2017 to 2018
    B. Health and Welfare; 2017 to 2018
    C. Education and Development; 2019 to 2020
    D. Human Resources; 2019 to 2020

5. During the five-year period, the annual budget of the Department of Human Resources was GREATER than the annual budget for the Department of Conservation and Environment in _____ of the years.

    A. none   B. one   C. two   D. three

6. If the total City X budget increases at the same rate from 2021 to 2022 as it did from 2020 to 2021, the total City X budget for 2022 will be MOST NEARLY _____ million.

    A. $180   B. $200   C. $210   D. $215

TEST 8

DIRECTIONS: Each question or incomplete statement is followed by several suggested answers or completions. Select the one that BEST answers the question or completes the statement. *PRINT THE LETTER OF THE CORRECT ANSWER IN THE SPACE AT THE RIGHT.*

Questions 1-3.

DIRECTIONS: Questions 1 through 3 are to be answered SOLELY on the basis of the following information.

Assume that in order to encourage Program A, the State and Federal governments have agreed to make the following reimbursements for money spent on Program A, provided the unreimbursed balance is paid from City funds.

During Fiscal Year 2021-2022 - For the first $2 million expended, 50% Federal reimbursement and 30% State reimbursement; for the next $3 million, 40% Federal reimbursement and 20% State reimbursement; for the next $5 million, 20% Federal reimbursement and 10% State reimbursement. Above $10 million expended, no Federal or State reimbursement.

During Fiscal Year 2022-2023 - For the first $1 million expended, 30% Federal reimbursement and 20% State reimbursement; for the next $4 million, 15% Federal reimbursement and 10% State reimbursement. Above $5 million expended, no Federal or State reimbursement.

1. Assume that the Program A expenditures are such that the State reimbursement for Fiscal Year 2021-2022 will be $1 million.
   Then, the Federal reimbursement for Fiscal Year 2021-2022 will be

   A. $1,600,000   B. $1,800,000
   C. $2,000,000   D. $2,600,000

2. Assume that $8 million were to be spent on Program A in Fiscal Year 2022-2023.
   The TOTAL amount of unreimbursed City funds required would be

   A. $3,500,000   B. $4,500,000
   C. $5,500,000   D. $6,500,000

3. Assume that the City desires to have a combined total of $6 million spent in Program A during both the Fiscal Year 2021-2022 and the Fiscal Year 2022-2023.
   Of the following expenditure combinations, the one which results in the GREATEST reimbursement of City funds is _____ in Fiscal Year 2021-2022 and _____ in Fiscal Year 2022-2023.

   A. $5 million; $1 million   B. $4 million; $2 million
   C. $3 million; $3 million   D. $2 million; $4 million

KEY (CORRECT ANSWERS)

TEST 1

1. D
2. C
3. C

TEST 2

1. B
2. A
3. A
4. D

TEST 3

1. A
2. D
3. B

TEST 4

1. A
2. B
3. C
4. C

TEST 5

1. A
2. C
3. C

TEST 6

1. C
2. D
3. A

TEST 7

1. D
2. A
3. A
4. B
5. B
6. D

TEST 8

1. B
2. D
3. A

PREPARING WRITTEN MATERIAL

PARAGRAPH REARRANGEMENT
COMMENTARY

The sentences that follow are in scrambled order. You are to rearrange them in proper order and indicate the letter choice containing the correct answer at the space at the right.

Each group of sentences in this section is actually a paragraph presented in scrambled order. Each sentence in the group has a place in that paragraph; no sentence is to be left out. You are to read each group of sentences and decide upon the best order in which to put the sentences so as to form a well-organized paragraph.

The questions in this section measure the ability to solve a problem when all the facts relevant to its solution are not given.

More specifically, certain positions of responsibility and authority require the employee to discover connection between events sometimes, apparently, unrelated. In order to do this, the employee will find it necessary to correctly infer that unspecified events have probably occurred or are likely to occur. This ability becomes especially important when action must be taken on incomplete information.

Accordingly, these questions require competitors to choose among several suggested alternatives, each of which presents a different sequential arrangement of the events. Competitors must choose the MOST logical of the suggested sequences.

In order to do so, they may be required to draw on general knowledge to infer missing concepts or events that are essential to sequencing the given events. Competitors should be careful to infer only what is essential to the sequence. The plausibility of the wrong alternatives will always require the inclusion of unlikely events or of additional chains of events which are NOT essential to sequencing the given events.

It's very important to remember that you are looking for the best of the four possible choices, and that the best choice of all may not even be one of the answers you're given to choose from.

There is no one right way to solve these problems. Many people have found it helpful to first write out the order of the sentences, as they would have arranged them, on their scrap paper before looking at the possible answers. If their optimum answer is there, this can save them some time. If it isn't, this method can still give insight into solving the problem. Others find it most helpful to just go through each of the possible choices, contrasting each as they go along. You should use whatever method feels comfortable and works for you.

While most of these types of questions are not that difficult, we've added a higher percentage of the difficult type, just to give you more practice. Usually there are only one or two questions on this section that contain such subtle distinctions that you're unable to answer confidently. And you then may find yourself stuck deciding between two possible choices, neither of which you're sure about.

EXAMINATION SECTION

TEST 1

DIRECTIONS: The sentences that follow are in scrambled order. You are to rearrange them in proper order and indicate the letter choice containing the correct answer. *PRINT THE LETTER OF THE CORRECT ANSWER IN THE SPACE AT THE RIGHT.*

1. Below are four statements labeled W, X, Y and Z. 1._____
   W. He was a strict and fanatic drillmaster.
   X. The word is always used in a derogatory sense and generally shows resentment and anger on the part of the user.
   Y. It is from the name of this Frenchman that we derive our English word, martinet.
   Z. Jean Martinet was the Inspector-General of Infantry during the reign of King Louis XIV.
   The PROPER order in which these sentences should be placed in a paragraph is:
   A. X, Z, W, Y   B. X, Z, Y, W   C. Z, W, Y, X   D. Z, Y, W, X

2. In the following paragraph, the sentences, which are numbered, have been 2._____
   jumbled.
   I. Since then it has undergone changes.
   II. It was incorporated in 1955 under the laws of the State of New York.
   III. Its primary purposes, a cleaner city, has, however, remained the same.
   IV. The Citizens Committee works in cooperation with the Mayor's Inter- 3._____
   departmental Committee for a Clean City.
   The order in which these sentences should be arranged to form a well-organized paragraph is:
   A. II, IV, I, III   B. III, IV, I, II   C. IV, II, I, III   D. IV, III, II, I

Questions 3-5.

DIRECTIONS: The sentences listed below are part of a meaningful paragraph but they are not given in their proper order. You are to decide what would be the BEST order in which to put the sentences so as to form a well-organized paragraph. Each sentence has a place in the paragraph; there are no extra sentences. You are then to answer Questions 3 through 5 inclusive on the basis of your rearrangements of these scrambled sentences into a properly organized paragraph.

In 1887 some insurance companies organized an Inspection Department to advise their clients on all phases of fire prevention and protection. Probably this has been due to the smaller annual fire losses in Great Britain than in the United States. It tests various fire prevention devices and appliances and determines manufacturing hazards and their safeguards. Fire research began earlier in the United States and is more advanced than in Great Britain. Later they established a laboratory specializing in electrical, mechanical, hydraulic, and chemical fields.

3. When the five sentences are arranged in proper order, the paragraph starts with the sentence which begins
   A. "In 1887…"   B. "Probably this…"   C. "It tests…"
   D. "Fire research…"   E. "Later they…"

4. In the last sentence listed above, "they" refers to
   A. the insurance companies   B. the United States and Great Britain
   C. the Inspection Department   D. clients
   E. technicians

5. When the above paragraph is properly arranged, it ends with the words
   A. "…and protection."   B. "…the United States."
   C. "…their safeguards."   D. "…in Great Britain."
   E. "…chemical fields."

KEY (CORRECT ANSWERS)

1. C
2. C
3. D
4. A
5. C

TEST 2

DIRECTIONS: In each of the questions numbered I through V, several sentences are given. For each question, choose as your answer the group of number that represents the MOST logical order of these sentences if they were arranged in paragraph form. *PRINT THE LETTER OF THE CORRECT ANSWER IN THE SPACE AT THE RIGHT.*

1. I. It is established when one shows that the landlord has prevented the tenant's enjoyment of his interest in the property leased.
    II. Constructive eviction is the result of a breach of the covenant of quiet enjoyment implied in all leases.
    III. In some parts of the United States, it is not complete until the tenant vacates within a reasonable time.
    IV. Generally, the acts must be of such serious and permanent character as to deny the tenant the enjoyment of his possessing rights.
    V. In this event, upon abandonment of the premises, the tenant's liability for that ceases.
    The CORRECT answer is:
    A. II, I, IV, III, V
    B. V, II, III, I, IV
    C. IV, III, I, II, V
    D. I, III, V, IV, II

    1.____

2. I. The powerlessness before private and public authorities that is the typical experience of the slum tenant is reminiscent of the situation of blue-collar workers all through the nineteenth century.
    II. Similarly, in recent years, this chapter of history has been reopened by anti-poverty groups which have attempted to organize slum tenants to enable them to bargain collectively with their landlords about the conditions of their tenancies.
    III. It is familiar history that many of the worker remedied their condition by joining together and presenting their demands collectively.
    IV. Like the workers, tenants are forced by the conditions of modern life into substantial dependence on these who possess great political aid and economic power.
    V. What's more, the very fact of dependence coupled with an absence of education and self-confidence makes them hesitant and unable to stand up for what they need from those in power.
    The CORRECT answer is:
    A. V, IV, I, II, III
    B. II, III, I, V, IV
    C. III, I, V, IV, II
    D. I, IV, V, III, II

    2.____

3. I. A railroad, for example, when not acting as a common carrier may contract away responsibility for its own negligence.
    II. As to a landlord, however, no decision has been found relating to the legal effect of a clause shifting the statutory duty of repair to the tenant.
    III. The courts have not passed on the validity of clauses relieving the landlord of this duty and liability.
    IV. They have, however, upheld the validity of exculpatory clauses in other types of contracts.

    3.____

V. Housing regulations impose a duty upon the landlord to maintain leased premises in safe condition.
VI. As another example, a bailee may limit his liability except for gross negligence, willful acts, or fraud.

The CORRECT answer is:
A. II, I, VI, IV, III, V
B. I, III, IV, V, VI, II
C. III, V, I, IV, II, VI
D. V, III, IV, I, VI, II

4.
I. Since there are only samples in the building, retail or consumer sales are generally eschewed by mart occupants, and in some instances, rigid controls are maintained to limit entrance to the mart only to those persons engaged in retailing.
II. Since World War I, in many larger cities, there has developed a new type of property, called the mart building.
III. It can, therefore, be used by wholesalers and jobbers for the display of sample merchandise.
IV. This type of building is most frequently a multi-storied, finished interior property which is a cross between a retail arcade and a loft building.
V. This limitation enables the mart occupants to ship the orders from another location after the retailer or dealer makes his selection from the samples.

The CORRECT answer is:
A. II, IV, III, I, V
B. IV, III, V, I, II
C. I, III, II, IV, V
D. I, IV, II, III, V

5.
I. In general, staff-line friction reduces the distinctive contribution of staff personnel.
II. The conflicts, however, introduce an uncontrolled element into the managerial system.
III. On the other hand, the natural resistance of the line to staff innovations probably usefully restrains over-eager efforts to apply untested procedures on a large scale.
IV. Under such conditions, it is difficult to know when valuable ideas are being sacrificed.
V. The relatively weak position of staff, requiring accommodation to the line, tends to restrict their ability to engage in free, experimental innovation.

The CORRECT answer is:
A. IV, II, III, I, V
B. I, V, III, II, IV
C. V, III, I, II, IV
D. II, I, IV, V, III

KEY (CORRECT ANSWERS)

1. A
2. D
3. D
4. A
5. B

TEST 3

DIRECTIONS: Questions 1 through 4 consist of six sentences which can be arranged in a logical sequence. For each question, select the choice which places the numbered sentences in the MOST logical sequent. *PRINT THE LETTER OF THE CORRECT ANSWER IN THE SPACE AT THE RIGHT.*

1. I. The burden of proof as to each issue is determined before trial and remains upon the same party throughout the trial.
    II. The jury is at liberty to believe one witness' testimony as against a number of contradictory witnesses.
    III. In a civil case, the party bearing the burden of proof is required to prove his contention by a fair preponderance of the evidence.
    IV. However, it must be noted that a fair preponderance of evidence does not necessarily mean a greater number of witnesses.
    V. The burden of proof is the burden which rests upon one of the parties to an action to persuade the trier of the facts, generally the jury, that a proposition he asserts is true.
    VI. If the evidence is equally balanced, or if it leaves the jury in such doubt as to be unable to decide the controversy either way, judgment must be given against the party upon whom the burden of proof rests.

    The CORRECT answer is:
    A. III, II, V, IV, I, VI
    B. I, II, VI, V, III, IV
    C. III, IV, V, I, II, VI
    D. V, I, III, VI, IV, II

    1.____

2. I. If a parent is without assets and is unemployed, he cannot be convicted of the crime of non-support of a child.
    II. The term "sufficient ability" has been held to mean sufficient financial ability.
    III. It does not matter if his unemployment is by choice or unavoidable circumstances.
    IV. If he fails to take any steps at all, he may be liable to prosecution for endangering the welfare of a child.
    V. Under the penal law, a parent is responsible for the support of his minor child only if the parent is "of sufficient ability."
    VI. An indigent parent may meet his obligation by borrowing money or by seeking aid under the provisions of the Social Welfare Law.

    The CORRECT answer is:
    A. VI, I, V, III, II, IV
    B. I, III, V, II, IV, VI
    C. V, II, I, III, VI, IV
    D. I, VI, IV, V, II, III

    2.____

3. I. Consider, for example, the case of a rabble rouser who urges a group of twenty people to go out and break the windows of a nearby factory.
    II. Therefore, the law fills the indicated gap with the crime of inciting to riot.
    III. A person is considered guilty of inciting to riot when he urges ten or more persons to engage in tumultuous and violent conduct of a kind likely to create public alarm.
    IV. However, if he has not obtained the cooperation of at least four people, he cannot be charged with unlawful assembly.

    3.____

77

V. The charge of inciting to riot was added to the law to cover types of conduct which cannot be classified as either the crime of "riot" or the crime of "unlawful assembly."
VI. If he acquires the acquiescence of at least four of them, he is guilty of unlawful assembly even if the project does not materialize.

The CORRECT answer is:
A. III, V, I, VI, IV, II
B. V, I, IV, VI, II, III
C. III, IV, I, V, II, VI
D. V, I, IV, VI, III, II

4.
I. If, however, the rebuttal evidence presents an issue of credibility, it is for the jury to determine whether the presumption has, in fact, been destroyed.
II. Once sufficient evidence to the contrary is introduced, the presumption disappears from the trial.
III. The effect of a presumption is to place the burden upon the adversary to come forward with evidence to rebut the presumption.
IV. When a presumption is overcome and ceases to exist in the case, the fact or facts which gave rise to the presumption still remain.
V. Whether a presumption has been overcome is ordinarily a question for the court.
VI. Such information may furnish a basis for a logical inference.

The CORRECT answer is:
A. IV, VI, II, V, I, III
B. III, II, V, I, IV, VI
C. V, III, VI, IV, II, I
D. V, IV, I, II, VI, III

KEY (CORRECT ANSWERS)

1. D
2. C
3. A
4. B

PREPARING WRITTEN MATERIALS
EXAMINATION SECTION
TEST 1

DIRECTIONS: Each question contains a sentence. Read each sentence carefully to decide whether it is correct. Then, in the space at the right, mark your answer:
- A. If the sentence is incorrect because of bad grammar or sentence structure;
- B. If the sentence is incorrect because of bad punctuation
- C. If the sentence is incorrect because of bad capitalization
- D. If the sentence is correct.

Each incorrect sentence has only one type of error. Consider a sentence correct if it has no errors, although there may be other correct ways of saying the same thing.

SAMPLE QUESTION i: One of our clerks were promoted yesterday.

The subject of this sentence is *one*, so the verb should be *was promoted* instead of *were promoted*. Since the sentence is incorrect because of bad grammar, the answer to Sample Question I is A.

SAMPLE QUESTION II: Between you and me, I would prefer not going there.

Since this sentence is correct, the answer to Sample Question II is D.

1. The National alliance of Businessmen is trying to persuade private businesses to hire youth in the summertime.   1.____

2. The supervisor who is on vacation, is in charge of processing vouchers.   2.____

3. The activity of the committee at its conferences is always stimulating.   3.____

4. After checking the addresses again, the letters went to the mailroom.   4.____

5. The director, as well as the employees, are interested in sharing the dividends.   5.____

6. The experiments conducted by professor Alford were described at a recent meeting of our organization.   6.____

7. I shall be glad to discuss these matters with whoever represents the Municipal Credit Union.   7.____

8. In my opinion, neither Mr. Price nor Mr. Roth knows how to operate this office appliance.   8.____

79

9. The supervisor, as well as the other stenographers, were unable to transcribe Miss Johnson's shorthand notes. 9.____

10. Important functions such as, recruiting and training, are performed by our unit. 10.____

11. Realizing that many students are interested in this position, we sent announcements to all the High Schools. 11.____

12. After pointing out certain incorrect conclusions, the report was revised by Mr. Clark and submitted to Mr. Batson. 12.____

13. The employer contributed two hundred dollars; the employees, one hundred dollars. 13.____

14. He realized that the time, when a supervisor could hire and fire, was over. 14.____

15. The complaints received by Commissioner Regan was the cause of the change in policy. 15.____

16. Any report, that is to be sent to the Federal Security Administration, must be approved and signed by Mr. Yound. 16.____

17. Of the two stenographers, Miss Rand is the more accurate. 17.____

18. Since the golf courses are crowded during the summer, more men are needed to maintain the courses in good playing condition. 18.____

19. Although he invited Mr. Frankel and I to attend a meeting of the Civil Service Assembly, we were unable to accept his invitation. 19.____

20. Only the employees who worked overtime last week may leave one hour earlier today. 20.____

21. We need someone who can speak french fluently. 21.____

22. A tall, elderly, man entered the office and asked to see Mr. Brown. 22.____

23. The clerk insisted that he had filed the correspondence in the proper cabinet. 23.____

24. "Will you assist us," he asked? 24.____

25. According to the information contained in the report, a large quantity of paper and envelopes were used by this bureau last year. 25.____

KEY (CORRECT ANSWERS)

1.	C		11.	C
2.	B		12.	A
3.	D		13.	D
4.	A		14.	B
5.	A		15.	A
6.	C		16.	B
7.	D		17.	D
8.	D		18.	C
9.	A		19.	A
10.	B		20.	D

21. C
22. B
23. D
24. B
25. A

TEST 2

DIRECTIONS: Each question consists of a sentence which may be classified appropriately under one of the following four categories:
   A. Incorrect because of faulty grammar or sentence structure.
   B. Incorrect because of faulty punctuation.
   C. Incorrect because of faulty capitalization.
   D. Correct

Examine each sentence carefully. Then, in the space at the right, print the capital letter preceding the option which is the BEST of the four suggested above. All incorrect sentences contain only one type of error. Consider a sentence correct if it contains none of the types of errors mentioned, although there may be other correct ways of expressing the same thought.

1. Mrs. Black the supervisor of the unit, has many important duties. 1.____
2. We spoke to the man whom you saw yesterday. 2.____
3. When a holiday falls on sunday, it is officially celebrated on monday. 3.____
4. Of the two reports submitted, this one is the best. 4.____
5. Each staff member, including the accountants, were invited to the meeting. 5.____
6. Give the package to whomever calls for it. 6.____
7. To plan the work is our responsibility; to carry it out is his. 7.____
8. "May I see the person in charge of this office," asked the visitor? 8.____
9. He knows that it was not us who prepared the report. 9.____
10. These problems were brought to the attention of senator Johnson. 10.____
11. The librarian classifies all books periodicals and documents. 11.____
12. Any employee who uses an adding machine realizes its importance. 12.____
13. Instead of coming to the office, the clerk should of come to the supply room. 13.____
14. He asked, "will your staff assist us?" 14.____
15. Having been posted on the bulletin board, we were certain that the announcements would be read. 15.____
16. He was not informed, that he would have to work overtime. 16.____
17. The wind blew several paper off of his desk. 17.____

18. Charles Dole, who is a member of the committee, was asked to confer with commissioner Wilson. 18._____

19. Miss Bell will issue a copy to whomever asks for one. 19._____

20. Most employees, and he is no exception do not like to work overtime. 20._____

21. This is the man whom you interviewed last week. 21._____

22. Of the two cities visited, White Plains is the cleanest. 22._____

23. Although he was willing to work on other holidays, he refused to work on Labor day. 23._____

24. If an employee wishes to attend the conference, he should fill out the necessary forms. 24._____

25. The division chief reports that an engineer and an inspector is needed for this special survey. 25._____

KEY (CORRECT ANSWERS)

1. B
2. D
3. C
4. A
5. A

6. A
7. D
8. B
9. A
10. C

11. B
12. D
13. A
14. C
15. A

16. B
17. A
18. C
19. A
20. B

21. D
22. A
23. C
24. D
25. A

TEST 3

DIRECTIONS: Each question consists of a sentence which may be classified appropriately under one of the following four categories:
- A. Incorrect because of faulty grammar or sentence structure.
- B. Incorrect because of faulty punctuation.
- C. Incorrect because of faulty capitalization.
- D. Correct

Examine each sentence carefully. Then, in the space at the right, print the capital letter preceding the option which is the BEST of the four suggested above. All incorrect sentences contain only one type of error. Consider a sentence correct if it contains none of the types of errors mentioned, although there may be other correct ways of expressing the same thought.

1. We have learned that there was more than twelve people present at the meeting.   1._____

2. Every one of the employees is able to do this kind of work.   2._____

3. Neither the supervisor nor his assistant are in the office today.   3._____

4. The office manager announced that any clerk, who volunteered for the assignment, would be rewarded.   4._____

5. After looking carefully in all the files, the letter was finally found on a desk.   5._____

6. In answer to the clerk's question, the supervisor said, "this assignment must be completed today."   6._____

7. The office manager says that he can permit only you and me to go to the meeting.   7._____

8. The supervisor refused to state who he would assign to the reception unit.   8._____

9. At the last meeting, he said that he would interview us in september.   9._____

10. Mr. Jones, who is one of our most experienced employees has been placed in charge of the main office.   10._____

11. I think that this adding machine is the most useful of the two we have in our office.   11._____

12. Between you and I, our new stenographer is not as competent as our former stenographer.   12._____

13. The new assignment should be given to whoever can do the work rapidly   13._____

14. Mrs. Smith, as well as three other typists, was assigned to the new office.   14._____

15. The staff assembled for the conference on time but, the main speaker arrived late.   15.____

16. The work was assigned to Miss Green and me.   16.____

17. The staff regulations state that an employee, who is frequently tardy, may receive a negative evaluation.   17.____

18. He is the kind of person who is always willing to undertake difficult assignments.   18.____

19. Mr. Wright's request cannot be granted under no conditions.   19.____

20. George Colt a new employee, was asked to deliver the report to the Domestic Relations Court.   20.____

21. The supervisor entered the room and said, "The work must be completed today."   21.____

22. The employees were given their assignments and, they were asked to begin work immediately.   22.____

23. The letter will be sent to the United States senate this week.   23.____

24. When the supervisor entered the room, he noticed that the book was laying on the desk.   24.____

25. The price of the pens were higher than the price of the pencils.   25.____

KEY (CORRECT ANSWERS)

1.	A		11.	A
2.	D		12.	A
3.	A		13.	D
4.	B		14.	D
5.	A		15.	B
6.	C		16.	D
7.	D		17.	B
8.	A		18.	D
9.	C		19.	A
10.	B		20.	B

21. D
22. B
23. C
24. A
25. A

EXAMINATION SECTION

TEST 1

DIRECTIONS: Each question or incomplete statement is followed by several suggested answers or completions. Select the one that BEST answers the question or completes the statement. *PRINT THE LETTER OF THE CORRECT ANSWER IN THE SPACE AT THE RIGHT.*

1. The one of the following which is the CHIEF reason for the difference between the administration of justice agencies and that of other units in public administration is that
   A. correctional institutions are concerned with security
   B. some defendants are proven to be innocent after trial
   C. the administration of justice is more complicated than other aspects of public administration
   D. correctional institutions produce services their clients or customers fail to understand or ask for

   1.____

2. Of the following, the MOST important reason why employees resist change is that
   A. they have not received adequate training in preparation for the change
   B. experience has shown that when new ideas don't work, employees get blamed and not the individuals responsible for the new ideas
   C. new ideas and methods almost always represent a threat to the security of the individuals involved
   D. new ideas often are not practical and disrupt operations unnecessarily

   2.____

3. Stress situations are ideal for building up a backlog of knowledge about an employee's behavior. Not only does it inform the supervisor of many aspects of a person's behavior patterns, but it is also vitally important to have foreknowledge of how people behave under stress.
   The one of the following which is NOT implied by this passage is that
   A. a person under stress may give some indication of his unsuitability for work in an institution
   B. putting people under stress is the best means of determining their usual patterns of behavior
   C. stress situations may give important clues about performance in the service
   D. there is a need to know about a person's reaction to situations *when the chips are down*

   3.____

4. There are situations requiring a supervisor to give direct orders to subordinates assigned to work under the direct control of other supervisors.
   Under which of the following conditions would this shift of command responsibility be MOST appropriate?
   A. Emergency operations require the cooperative action of two or more organizational units.

   4.____

B. One of the other supervisors is not doing his job, thus defeating the goals of the organization.
C. The subordinates are performing their assigned tasks in the absence of their own supervisor.
D. The subordinates ask a superior officer who is not their own supervisor how to perform an assignment given them by their supervisor.

5. The one of the following which BEST differentiates staff supervision from line supervision is that
   A. staff supervision has the authority to immediately correct a line subordinate's action
   B. staff supervision is an advisory relationship
   C. line supervision goes beyond the normal boundaries of direct supervision within a command
   D. line supervision does not report findings and make recommendations

6. Decision-making is a rational process calling for a *suspended judgment* by the supervisor until all the facts have been ascertained and analyzed, and the consequences of alternative courses of action studied; then the decision maker
   A. acts as both judge and jury and selects what he believes to be the best of the alternative plans
   B. consults with those who will be most directly involved to obtain a recommendation as to the most appropriate course of action
   C. reviews the facts which he has already analyzed, reduces his thoughts to writing, and selects that course of action which can have the fewest negative consequences if his thinking contains an error
   D. stops, considers the matter for at least a 24-hour period, before referring it to a superior for evaluation

7. Decision-making can be defined as the
   A. delegation of authority and responsibility to persons capable of performing their assigned duties with moderate or little supervision
   B. imposition of a supervisor's decision upon a work group
   C. technique of selecting the course of action with the most desired consequences, and the least undesired or unexpected consequence
   D. process principally concerned with improvement of procedures

8. A supervisor who is not well-motivated and has no desire to accept basic responsibilities will
   A. compromise to the extent of permitting poor performance for lengthy periods without correction
   B. get good performance from his work group if the employees are satisfied with their pay and other working conditions
   C. not have marginal workers in his work group if the work is interesting
   D. perform adequately as long as the work of his group consists of routine operations

9. A supervisor is more than a bond or connecting link between two levels of employees. He has joint responsibility which must be shared with both management and with the work group.
Of the following, the item which BEST expresses the meaning of this statement is:
   A. A supervisor works with both management and the work group and must reconcile the differences between them.
   B. In management, the supervisor is solely concerned with efforts directing the work of his subordinates.
   C. The supervisory role is basically that of a liaison man between management and the work force.
   D. What a supervisor says and does when confronted with day-to-day problems depends upon is level in the organization.

9.____

10. Operations research is the observation of operations in business or government, and it utilizes both hypotheses and controlled experiments to determine the outcome of decisions. In effect, it reproduces the future impact on the decision in a clinical environment suited to intensive study.
Operations research has
   A. been more promising than applied research in the ascertaining of knowledge for the purpose of decision-making
   B. never been amenable to fact analysis on the grand scale
   C. not been used extensively in government
   D. proven to be the only rational and logical approach to decision-making on long-range problems

10.____

11. Assume that a civilian makes a complaint regarding the behavior of a certain worker to the supervisor of the worker. The supervisor regards the complaint as unjustified and unreasonable.
In this circumstances, the supervisor
   A. must make a written note of the complaint and forward it through channels to the unit or individual responsible for complaint investigations
   B. should assure the complainant that disciplinary action will be appropriate to the seriousness of the alleged offense
   C. should immediately summon the worker if he is available so that the latter may attempt to straighten out the difficulty
   D. should inform the complainant that his complaint appears to be unjustified and unreasonable

11.____

12. Modern management usually establishes a personal history folder for an employee at the time of hiring. Disciplinary matters appear in such personal history folders. Employees do not like the idea of disciplinary actions appearing in their permanent personal folders.
Authorities believe that
   A. after a few years have passed since the commission of the infraction, disciplinary actions should be removed from folders
   B. disciplinary actions should remain in folders; it is not the records but the use of records that requires detailed study

12.____

C. most personnel have not had disciplinary action taken against them and would resent the removal of disciplinary actions for such folders
D. there is no point in removing disciplinary actions from personal history folders since employees who have been guilty of infractions should not be allowed to forget their infractions

13. While supervisors should not fear the acceptance of responsibility, they
    A. generally seek out responsibility that subordinates should exercise, particularly when the supervisors do not have sufficient work to do
    B. must be on guard against the abuse of authority that often accompanies the acceptance of total responsibility
    C. should avoid responsibility that is customarily exercised by their superiors
    D. who are anxious for promotions accept responsibility but do not exercise the authority warranted by the responsibility

14. Planning is part of the decision-making process. By planning is meant the development of details of alternative plans of action.
    The key to *effective* planning is
    A. careful research to determine whether a tentative plan has been tried at some time in the past
    B. participation by employees in planning, preferably those employees who will be involved in putting the selected plan into action
    C. speed; poor plans can be discarded after they are put into effect while good plans usually are not put into effect because of delays
    D. writing the plan up in considerable detail and then forwarding the plan, through channels, to the executive officer having final approval of the plan

15. Equating strict discipline with punitive measures and lax discipline with rehabilitation creates a false dichotomy.
    The one of the statements given below that would BEST follow from the belief expressed in this statement is that discipline
    A. is important for treatment
    B. militates against treatment programs
    C. is not an important consideration in institutions where effective rehabilitation programs prevail
    D. minimizes the need for punitive measures if it is strict

16. If training starts at the lower level of command, it is like planting a seed in tilled ground but removing the sun and rain. Seeds cannot grow unless they have help from above.
    Of the following, the MOST appropriate conclusion to be drawn from this statement is that
    A. the head of an institution may not delegate authority for the planning of an institutional training program for staff
    B. on-the-job training is better than formalized training courses
    C. regularly scheduled training courses must be planned in advance
    D. staff training is the responsibility of higher levels of comman

17. The one of the following that BEST describes the meaning of *in-service staff training* is:
    A. The training of personnel who are below average in performance
    B. The training given to each employee throughout his employment
    C. The training of staff only in their own specialized fields
    D. Classroom training where the instructor and employees develop a positive and productive relationship leading to improved efficiency on the job

18. All bureau personnel should be concerned about, and involved in, public relations.
    Of the following, the MOST important reason for this statement is that
    A. an institution is an agency of the government supported by public funds and responsible to the public
    B. institutions are places of public business and, therefore, the public is interested in them
    C. some personnel need publicity in order to advance
    D. personnel sometimes need publicity in order to ensure that their grievances are acted upon by higher authority

19. The MOST important factor in establishing a disciplinary policy in an organization is
    A. consistency of application
    B. strict supervisors
    C. strong enforcement
    D. the degree of toughness or laxity

20. The FIRST step in planning a program is to
    A. clearly define the objectives
    B. estimate the costs
    C. hire a program director
    D. solicit funds

21. The PRIMARY purpose of control in an organization is to
    A. punish those who do not do their job well
    B. get people to do what is necessary to achieve an objective
    C. develop clearly stated rules and regulations
    D. regulate expenditures

22. The UNDERLYING principle of *sound* administration is to
    A. base administration on investigation of facts
    B. have plenty of resources available
    C. hire a strong administrator
    D. establish a broad policy

23. An IMPORTANT aspect to keep in mind during the decision-making process is that
    A. all possible alternatives for attaining goals should be sought out and considered
    B. considering various alternatives only leads to confusion
    C. once a decision has been made, it cannot be retracted
    D. there is only one correct method to reach any goal

24. Implementation of accountability requires
    A. a leader who will not hesitate to take punitive action
    B. an established system of communication from the bottom to the top
    C. explicit directives from leaders
    D. too much expense to justify it

    24.____

25. The CHIEF danger of a decentralized control system is that
    A. excessive reports and communications will be generated
    B. problem areas may not be detected readily
    C. the expense will become prohibitive
    D. this will result in too many *chiefs*

    25.____

KEY (CORRECT ANSWERS)

1.	D		11.	D
2.	C		12.	A
3.	B		13.	B
4.	A		14.	B
5.	B		15.	A
6.	A		16.	D
7.	C		17.	B
8.	A		18.	A
9.	A		19.	A
10.	C		20.	A

21. B
22. A
23. A
24. B
25. B

TEST 2

DIRECTIONS: Each question or incomplete statement is followed by several suggested answers or completions. Select the one that BEST answers the question or completes the statement. *PRINT THE LETTER OF THE CORRECT ANSWER IN THE SPACE AT THE RIGHT.*

1. When giving orders to his subordinates, a certain supervisor often includes information as to why the work is necessary.
   This approach by the supervisor is GENERALLY
   A. *inadvisable*, since it appears that he is avoiding responsibility and wishes to blame his superiors
   B. *inadvisable*, since it creates the impression that he is trying to impress the subordinates with his importance
   C. *advisable*, since it serves to motivate the subordinates by giving them a reason for wanting to do the work
   D. *advisable*, since it shows that he is knowledgeable and is in control of his assignments

1.____

2. Some supervisors often ask capable, professional subordinates to get some work done with questions such as: *Mary, would you try to complete that work today?*
   The use of such request orders USUALLY
   A. gets results which are as good as or better than results from direct orders
   B. shows the supervisor to be weak and lowers the respect of his subordinates
   C. provokes resentment as compared to the use of direct orders
   D. leads to confusion as to the proper procedure to follow when carrying out orders

2.____

3. Assume that a supervisor, because of an emergency when time was essential, and in the absence of his immediate superior, went out of the chain of command to get a decision from a higher level.
   It would consequently be MOST appropriate for the immediate superior to
   A. reprimand him for his action, since the long-range consequences are far more detrimental than the immediate gain
   B. encourage him to use this method, since the chain of command is an outmoded and discredited system which inhibits productive work
   C. order him to refrain from any repetition of this action in the future
   D. support him as long as he informed the superior of the action at the earliest opportunity

3.____

4. A supervisor gave instructions which he knew were somewhat complex to a subordinate. He then asked the subordinate to repeat the instructions to him.
   The supervisor's decision to have the subordinate repeat the instructions was
   A. *good practice*, mainly because the subordinate would realize the importance of carefully following instructions

4.____

B. *poor practice*, mainly because the supervisor should have given the employee time to ponder the instructions, and then, if necessary, to ask questions
C. *good practice*, mainly because the supervisor could see whether the subordinate had any apparent problem in understanding the instructions
D. *poor practice*, mainly because the subordinate should not be expected to have the same degree of knowledge as the supervisor

5. Supervisors and subordinates must successfully communicate with each other in order to work well together.
Which of the following statements concerning communication of this type is CORRECT?
   A. When speaking to his subordinates, a supervisor should make every effort to appear knowledgeable about all aspects of their work.
   B. Written communications should be prepared by the supervisor at his own level of comprehension.
   C. The average employee tends to give meaning to communication according to his personal interpretation.
   D. The effective supervisor communicates as much information as he has available to anyone who is interested.

5._____

6. A supervisor should be aware of situations in which it is helpful to put his orders to his subordinates in writing.
Which of the following situations would MOST likely call for a written order rather than an oral order?
The order
   A. gives complicated instructions which vary from ordinary practice
   B. involves the performance of duties for which the subordinate is responsible
   C. directs subordinates to perform duties similar to those which they performed in the recent past
   D. concerns a matter that must be promptly completed or dealt with

6._____

7. Assume that a supervisor discovers that a false rumor about possible layoffs has spread among his subordinates through the grapevine.
Of the following, the BEST way for the supervisor to deal with this situation is to
   A. use the grapevine to leak accurate information
   B. call a meeting to provide information and to answer questions
   C. post a notice on the bulletin board denying the rumor
   D. institute procedures designed to eliminate the grapevine

7._____

8. Communications in an organization with many levels becomes subject to different interpretations at each level and have a tendency to become distorted. The more levels there are in an organization, the greater the likelihood that the final recipient of a communication will get the wrong message.
The one of the following statements which BEST supports the foregoing viewpoint is:
   A. Substantial communications problems exist at high management levels in organizations.

8._____

B. There is a relationship in an organization between the number of hierarchical levels and interference with communications.
C. An opportunity should be given to subordinates at all levels to communicate their views with impunity.
D. In larger organizations, there tends to be more interference with downward communications than with upward communications.

9. A subordinate comes to you, his supervisor, to ask a detailed question about a new agency directive; however, you do not know the answer.
Of the following, the MOST helpful response to give the subordinate is to
   A. point out that since your own supervisor has failed to keep you informed of this matter, it is probably unimportant
   B. give the most logical interpretation you can, based on your best judgment
   C. ask him to raise the question with other supervisors until he finds one who knows the answer, then let you know also
   D. explain that you do not know and assure him that you will get the information for him

9.____

10. The traditional view of management theory is that communication in an organization should follow the table of organization. A newer theory holds that timely communication often requires bypassing certain steps in the hierarchical chain.
However, the MAIN advantage of using formal channels of communication within an organization is that
   A. an employee is thereby restricted in his relationships to his immediate superior and his immediate subordinates
   B. information is thereby transmitted to everyone who should be informed
   C. the organization will have an appeal channel, or a mechanism by which subordinates can go over their superior's head
   D. employees are thereby encouraged to exercise individual initiative

10.____

11. It is unfair to hold subordinates responsible for the performance of duties for which they do not have the requisite authority.
When this is done, it violates the principle that
   A. responsibility cannot be greater than that implied by delegated authority
   B. responsibility should be greater than that implied by delegated authority
   C. authority cannot be greater than that implied by delegated responsibility
   D. authority should be greater than that implied by delegated responsibility

11.____

12. Assume that a supervisor wishes to delegate some tasks to a capable subordinate.
It would be MOST in keeping with the principles of delegation for the supervisor to
   A. ask another supervisor who is experienced in the delegated tasks to evaluate the subordinate's work from time to time
   B. monitor continually the subordinate's performance by carefully reviewing his work

12.____

C. request experienced employees to submit peer ratings of the work of the subordinate
D. tell the subordinates what problems are likely to be encountered and specify which problems to report on

13. There are three types of leadership: *autocratic*, in which the leader makes the decisions and seeks compliance from his subordinates; *democratic*, in which the leader consults with his subordinate and lets them help set policy; and *free rein*, in which the leader acts as an information center and exercises minimum control over his subordinates.
A supervisor can be MOST effective if he decides to
    A. use democratic leadership techniques exclusively
    B. avoid the use of autocratic leadership techniques entirely
    C. employ the three types of leadership according to the situation
    D. rely mainly on autocratic leadership techniques

13.____

14. During a busy period of work, Employee A asked his supervisor for leave in order to take an ordinary vacation. The supervisor denied the request. The following day, Employee B asked for leave during the same period because his wife had just gone to the hospital for an indeterminate stay and he had family matters to tend to.
Of the following, the BEST way for the supervisor to deal with Employee B's request is to
    A. grant the request and give the reason to the other employee
    B. suggest that the employee make his request to higher management
    C. delay the request immediately since granting it would show favoritism
    D. defer any decision until the duration of the hospital stay is determined

14.____

15. Assume that you are a supervisor and that a subordinate tells you he has a grievance.
In general, you should FIRST
    A. move the grievance forward in order to get a prompt decision
    B. discourage this type of behavior on the part of subordinates
    C. attempt to settle the grievance
    D. refer the subordinate to the personnel office

15.____

16. A supervisor may have available a large variety of rewards he can use to motivate his subordinates. However, some supervisors choose the wrong rewards.
A supervisor is MOST likely to make such a mistake if he
    A. appeals to a subordinate's desire to be well regarded by his co-workers
    B. assumes that the subordinate's goals and preferences are the same as his own
    C. conducts in-depth discussions with a subordinate in order to discover his preference
    D. limits incentives to those rewards which he is authorized to provide or to recommend

16.____

17. Employee performance appraisal is open to many kinds of errors. When a supervisor is preparing such an appraisal, he is MOST likely to commit an error if
    A. employees are indifferent to the consequences of their performance appraisals
    B. the entire period for which the evaluation is being made is taken into consideration
    C. standard measurement criteria are used as performance benchmarks
    D. personal characteristics of employees which are not job-related are given weight

17.____

18. Assume that a supervisor finds that a report prepared by an employee is unsatisfactory and should be done over.
    Which of the following should the supervisor do?
    A. Give the report to another employee who can complete it properly
    B. Have the report done over by the same employee after successfully training him
    C. Hold a meeting to train all the employees so as not to single out the employee who performed unsatisfactory
    D. Accept the report so as not to discourage the employee and then make the corrections himself

18.____

19. Employees sometimes wish to have personal advice and counseling, in confidence, about their job-related problems. These problems may include such concerns as health matters, family difficulties, alcoholism, debts, emotional disturbances, etc.
    Such assistance is BEST provided through
    A. maintenance of an exit interview program to find reasons for, and solutions to, turn-over problems
    B. arrangements for employees to discuss individual problems informally outside normal administrative channels
    C. procedures which allow employees to submit anonymous inquiries to the personnel department
    D. special hearing committees consisting of top management in addition to immediate supervisors

19.____

20. An employee is always a member of some unit of the formal organization. He may also be a member of an informal work group.
    With respect to employee productivity and job satisfaction, the informal work group can MOST accurately be said to
    A. have no influence of any kind on its members
    B. influence its members negatively only
    C. influence its members positively only
    D. influence its members negatively or positively

20.____

21. In order to encourage employees to make suggestions, many public agencies have employee suggestion programs.
    What is the MAJOR benefit of such a program to the agency as a whole?

21.____

It
- A. brings existing or future problems to management's attention
- B. reduces the number of minor accidents
- C. requires employees to share in decision-making responsibilities
- D. reveals employees who have inadequate job knowledge

22. Assume that you have been asked to interview a seemingly shy applicant for a temporary position in your department.
For you to ask the kinds of questions that begin with *What, Where, Why, When, Who, and How,* is
- A. *good practice*; it informs the applicant that he must conform to the requirements of the department
- B. *poor practice*; it exceeds the extent and purpose of an initial interview
- C. *good practice*; it encourages the applicant to talk to a greater extent
- D. *poor practice*; it encourages the applicant to dominate the discussion

23. In recent years, job enlargement or job enrichment has tended to replace job simplification.
Those who advocate job enrichment or enlargement consider it *desirable* CHIEFLY because
- A. it allows supervisors to control closely the activities of subordinates
- B. it produces greater job satisfaction through reduction of responsibility
- C. most employees prefer to avoid work which is new and challenging
- D. positions with routinized duties are unlikely to provide job satisfaction

24. Job rotation is a training method in which an employee temporarily changes places with another employee of equal rank.
What is usually the MAIN purpose of job rotation? To
- A. politely remove the person being rotated from an unsuitable assignment
- B. increase skills and provide broader experience
- C. prepare the person being rotated for a permanent change
- D. test the skills of the person being rotated

25. There are several principles that a supervisor needs to know if he is to deal adequately with his training responsibilities.
Which of the following is usually NOT a principle of training?
- A. People should be trained according to their individual needs.
- B. People can learn by being told or shown how to do work but best of all by doing work under guidance.
- C. People can be easily trained even if they have no desire to learn.
- D. Training should be planned, scheduled, executed, and evaluated systematically.

KEY (CORRECT ANSWERS)

1.	C	11.	A
2.	A	12.	D
3.	D	13.	C
4.	C	14.	A
5.	C	15.	C
6.	A	16.	B
7.	B	17.	D
8.	B	18.	B
9.	D	19.	B
10.	B	20.	D

21.	A
22.	C
23.	D
24.	B
25.	C

PHILOSOPHY, PRINCIPLES, PRACTICES, AND TECHNICS OF SUPERVISION, ADMINISTRATION, MANAGEMENT, AND ORGANIZATION

TABLE OF CONTENTS

	Page
MEANING OF SUPERVISION	1
THE OLD AND THE NEW SUPERVISION	1
THE EIGHT (8) BASIC PRINCIPLES OF THE NEW SUPERVISION	1
I. Principle of Responsibility	1
II. Principle of Authority	2
III. Principle of Self-Growth	2
IV. Principle of Individual Worth	2
V. Principle of Creative Leadership	2
VI. Principle of Success and Failure	2
VII. Principle of Science	3
VIII. Principle of Cooperation	3
WHAT IS ADMINISTRATION?	3
I. Practices Commonly Classed as "Supervisory"	3
II. Practices Commonly Classed as "Administrative"	3
III. Practices Commonly Classed as Both "Supervisory" and "Administrative"	4
RESPONSIBILITIES OF THE SUPERVISOR	4
COMPETENCIES OF THE SUPERVISOR	4
THE PROFESSIONAL SUPERVISOR-EMPLOYEE RELATIONSHIP	4
MINI-TEXT IN SUPERVISION, ADMINISTRATION, MANAGEMENT, AND ORGANIZATION	5
I. Brief Highlights	5
A. Levels of Management	6
B. What the Supervisor Must Learn	6
C. A Definition of Supervision	6
D. Elements of the Team Concept	6
E. Principles of Organization	6
F. The Four Important Parts of Every Job	7
G. Principles of Delegation	7
H. Principles of Effective Communications	7
I. Principles of Work Improvement	7
J. Areas of Job Improvement	7
K. Seven Key Points in Making Improvements	8

	L.	Corrective Techniques for Job Improvement	8
	M.	A Planning Checklist	8
	N.	Five Characteristics of Good Directions	9
	O.	Types of Directions	9
	P.	Controls	9
	Q.	Orienting the New Employee	9
	R.	Checklist for Orienting New Employees	9
	S.	Principles of Learning	10
	T.	Causes of Poor Performance	10
	U.	Four Major Steps in On-the-Job Instructions	10
	V.	Employees Want Five Things	10
	W.	Some Don'ts in Regard to Praise	11
	X.	How to Gain Your Workers' Confidence	11
	Y.	Sources of Employee Problems	11
	Z.	The Supervisor's Key to Discipline	11
	AA.	Five Important Processes of Management	12
	BB.	When the Supervisor Fails to Plan	12
	CC.	Fourteen General Principles of Management	12
	DD.	Change	12
II.	Brief Topical Summaries		13
	A.	Who/What is the Supervisor?	13
	B.	The Sociology of Work	13
	C.	Principles and Practices of Supervision	14
	D.	Dynamic Leadership	14
	E.	Processes for Solving Problems	15
	F.	Training for Results	15
	G.	Health, Safety, and Accident Prevention	16
	H.	Equal Employment Opportunity	16
	I.	Improving Communications	16
	J.	Self-Development	17
	K.	Teaching and Training	17
		1. The Teaching Process	17
		a. Preparation	17
		b. Presentation	18
		c. Summary	18
		d. Application	18
		e. Evaluation	18
		2. Teaching Methods	18
		a. Lecture	18
		b. Discussion	18
		c. Demonstration	19
		d. Performance	19
		e. Which Method to Use	19

PHILOSOPHY, PRINCIPLES, PRACTICES, AND TECHNICS OF SUPERVISION, ADMINISTRATION, MANAGEMENT, AND ORGANIZATION

MEANING OF SUPERVISION

The extension of the democratic philosophy has been accompanied by an extension in the scope of supervision. Modern leaders and supervisors no longer think of supervision in the narrow sense of being confined chiefly to visiting employees, supplying materials, or rating the staff. They regard supervision as being intimately related to all the concerned agencies of society, they speak of the supervisor's function in terms of "growth," rather than the "improvement" of employees.

This modern concept of supervision may be defined as follows: Supervision is leadership and the development of leadership within groups which are cooperatively engaged in inspection, research, training, guidance, and evaluation.

THE OLD AND THE NEW SUPERVISION

TRADITIONAL
1. Inspection
2. Focused on the employee
3. Visitation
4. Random and haphazard
5. Imposed and authoritarian
6. One person usually

MODERN
1. Study and analysis
2. Focused on aims, materials, methods, supervisors, employees, environment
3. Demonstrations, intervisitation, workshops, directed reading, bulletins, etc.
4. Definitely organized and planned (scientific)
5. Cooperative and democratic
6. Many persons involved (creative)

THE EIGHT (8) BASIC PRINCIPLES OF THE NEW SUPERVISION

I. Principle of Responsibility
   Authority to act and responsibility for acting must be joined.
   A. If you give responsibility, give authority.
   B. Define employee duties clearly.
   C. Protect employees from criticism by others.
   D. Recognize the rights as well as obligations of employees.
   E. Achieve the aims of a democratic society insofar as it is possible within the area of your work.
   F. Establish a situation favorable to training and learning.
   G. Accept ultimate responsibility for everything done in your section, unit, office, division, department.
   H. Good administration and good supervision are inseparable.

II. Principle of Authority
The success of the supervisor is measured by the extent to which the power of authority is not used.
   A. Exercise simplicity and informality in supervision
   B. Use the simplest machinery of supervision
   C. If it is good for the organization as a whole, it is probably justified.
   D. Seldom be arbitrary or authoritative.
   E. Do not base your work on the power of position or of personality.
   F. Permit and encourage the free expression of opinions.

III. Principle of Self-Growth
The success of the supervisor is measured by the extent to which, and the speed with which, he is no longer needed.
   A. Base criticism on principles, not on specifics.
   B. Point out higher activities to employees.
   C. Train for self-thinking by employees to meet new situations.
   D. Stimulate initiative, self-reliance, and individual responsibility
   E. Concentrate on stimulating the growth of employees rather than on removing defects.

IV. Principle of Individual Worth
Respect for the individual is a paramount consideration in supervision.
   A. Be human and sympathetic in dealing with employees.
   B. Don't nag about things to be done.
   C. Recognize the individual differences among employees and seek opportunities to permit best expression of each personality.

V. Principle of Creative Leadership
The best supervision is that which is not apparent to the employee.
   A. Stimulate, don't drive employees to creative action.
   B. Emphasize doing good things.
   C. Encourage employees to do what they do best.
   D. Do not be too greatly concerned with details of subject or method.
   E. Do not be concerned exclusively with immediate problems and activities.
   F. Reveal higher activities and make them both desired and maximally possible.
   G. Determine procedures in the light of each situation but see that these are derived from a sound basic philosophy.
   H. Aid, inspire, and lead so as to liberate the creative spirit latent in all good employees.

VI. Principle of Success and Failure
There are no unsuccessful employees, only unsuccessful supervisors who have failed to give proper leadership.
   A. Adapt suggestions to the capacities, attitudes, and prejudices of employees.
   B. Be gradual, be progressive, be persistent.
   C. Help the employee find the general principle; have the employee apply his own problem to the general principle.
   D. Give adequate appreciation for good work and honest effort.
   E. Anticipate employee difficulties and help to prevent them.
   F. Encourage employees to do the desirable things they will do anyway.
   G. Judge your supervision by the results it secures.

VII. Principle of Science
Successful supervision is scientific, objective, and experimental. It is based on facts, not on prejudices.
A. Be cumulative in results.
B. Never divorce your suggestions from the goals of training.
C. Don't be impatient of results.
D. Keep all matters on a professional, not a personal, level.
E. Do not be concerned exclusively with immediate problems and activities.
F. Use objective means of determining achievement and rating where possible.

VIII. Principle of Cooperation
Supervision is a cooperative enterprise between supervisor and employee.
A. Begin with conditions as they are.
B. Ask opinions of all involved when formulating policies.
C. Organization is as good as its weakest link.
D. Let employees help to determine policies and department programs.
E. Be approachable and accessible—physically and mentally.
F. Develop pleasant social relationships.

WHAT IS ADMINISTRATION

Administration is concerned with providing the environment, the material facilities, and the operational procedures that will promote the maximum growth and development of supervisors and employees. (Organization is an aspect and a concomitant of administration.)

There is no sharp line of demarcation between supervision and administration; these functions are intimately interrelated and, often, overlapping. They are complementary activities.

I. Practices Commonly Classed as "Supervisory"
A. Conducting employees' conferences
B. Visiting sections, units, offices, divisions, departments
C. Arranging for demonstrations
D. Examining plans
E. Suggesting professional reading
F. Interpreting bulletins
G. Recommending in-service training courses
H. Encouraging experimentation
I. Appraising employee morale
J. Providing for intervisitation

II. Practices Commonly Classified as "Administrative"
A. Management of the office
B. Arrangement of schedules for extra duties
C. Assignment of rooms or areas
D. Distribution of supplies
E. Keeping records and reports
F. Care of audio-visual materials
G. Keeping inventory records
H. Checking record cards and books

I. Programming special activities
  J. Checking on the attendance and punctuality of employees

III. Practices Commonly Classified as Both "Supervisory" and "Administrative"
  A. Program construction
  B. Testing or evaluating outcomes
  C. Personnel accounting
  D. Ordering instructional materials

RESPONSIBILITIES OF THE SUPERVISOR

A person employed in a supervisory capacity must constantly be able to improve his own efficiency and ability. He represent the employer to the employees and only continuous self-examination can make him a capable supervisor.

Leadership and training are the supervisor's responsibility. An efficient working unit is one in which the employees work with the supervisor. It is his job to bring out the best in his employees. He must always be relaxed, courteous, and calm in his association with his employees. Their feelings are important, and a harsh attitude does not develop the most efficient employees.

COMPETENCES OF THE SUPERVISOR

  I. Complete knowledge of the duties and responsibilities of his position.
  II. To be able to organize a job, plan ahead, and carry through.
  III. To have self-confidence and initiative.
  IV. To be able to handle the unexpected situation and make quick decisions.
  V. To be able to properly train subordinates in the positions they are best suited for.
  VI. To be able to keep good human relations among his subordinates.
  VII. To be able to keep good human relations between his subordinates and himself and to earn their respect and trust.

THE PROFESSIONAL SUPERVISOR-EMPLOYEE RELATIONSHIP

There are two kinds of efficiency: one kind is only apparent and is produced in organizations through the exercise of mere discipline; this is but a simulation of the second, or true, efficiency which springs from spontaneous cooperation. If you are a manager, no matter how great or small your responsibility, it is your job, in the final analysis, to create and develop this involuntary cooperation among the people whom you supervise. For, no matter how powerful a combination of money, machines, and materials a company may have, this is a dead and sterile thing without a team of willing, thinking, and articulate people to guide it.

The following 21 points are presented as indicative of the exemplary basic relationship that should exist between supervisor and employee:

1. Each person wants to be liked and respected by his fellow employee and wants to be treated with consideration and respect by his superior.
2. The most competent employee will make an error. However, in a unit where good relations exist between the supervisor and his employees, tenseness and fear do not exist. Thus, errors are not hidden or covered up, and the efficiency of a unit is not impaired.

3. Subordinates resent rules, regulations, or orders that are unreasonable or unexplained.
4. Subordinates are quick to resent unfairness, harshness, injustices, and favoritism.
5. An employee will accept responsibility if he knows that he will be complimented for a job well done, and not too harshly chastised for failure; that his supervisor will check the cause of the failure, and, if it was the supervisor's fault, he will assume the blame therefore. If it was the employee's fault, his supervisor will explain the correct method or means of handling the responsibility.
6. An employee wants to receive credit for a suggestion he has made, that is used. If a suggestion cannot be used, the employee is entitled to an explanation. The supervisor should not say "no" and close the subject.
7. Fear and worry slow up a worker's ability. Poor working environment can impair his physical and mental health. A good supervisor avoids forceful methods, threats, and arguments to get a job done.
8. A forceful supervisor is able to train his employees individually and as a team, and is able to motivate them in the proper channels.
9. A mature supervisor is able to properly evaluate his subordinates and to keep them happy and satisfied.
10. A sensitive supervisor will never patronize his subordinates.
11. A worthy supervisor will respect his employees' confidences.
12. Definite and clear-cut responsibilities should be assigned to each executive.
13. Responsibility should always be coupled with corresponding authority.
14. No change should be made in the scope or responsibilities of a position without a definite understanding to that effect on the part of all persons concerned.
15. No executive or employee, occupying a single position in the organization, should be subject to definite orders from more than one source.
16. Orders should never be given to subordinates over the head of a responsible executive. Rather than do this, the officer in question should be supplanted.
17. Criticisms of subordinates should, whoever possible, be made privately, and in no case should a subordinate be criticized in the presence of executives or employees of equal or lower rank.
18. No dispute or difference between executives or employees as to authority or responsibilities should be considered too trivial for prompt and careful adjudication.
19. Promotions, wage changes, and disciplinary action should always be approved by the executive immediately superior to the one directly responsible.
20. No executive or employee should ever be required, or expected, to be at the same time an assistant to, and critic of, another.
21. Any executive whose work is subject to regular inspection should, wherever practicable, be given the assistance and facilities necessary to enable him to maintain an independent check of the quality of his work.

MINI-TEXT IN SUPERVISION, ADMINISTRATION, MANAGEMENT, AND ORGANIZATION

I. Brief Highlights

Listed concisely and sequentially are major headings and important data in the field for quick recall and review.

A. Levels of Management
Any organization of some size has several levels of management. In terms of a ladder, the levels are:

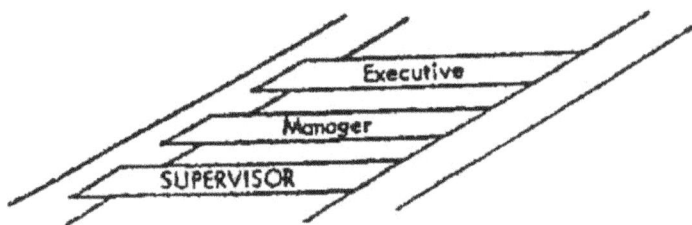

The first level is very important because it is the beginning point of management leadership.

B. What the Supervisor Must Learn
A supervisor must learn to:
1. Deal with people and their differences
2. Get the job done through people
3. Recognize the problems when they exist
4. Overcome obstacles to good performance
5. Evaluate the performance of people
6. Check his own performance in terms of accomplishment

C. A Definition of Supervisor
The term supervisor means any individual having authority, in the interests of the employer, to hire, transfer, suspend, lay-off, recall, promote, discharge, assign, reward, or discipline other employees or responsibility to direct them, or to adjust their grievances, or effectively to recommend such action, if, in connection with the foregoing, exercise of such authority is not of a merely routine or clerical nature but requires the use of independent judgment.

D. Elements of the Team Concept
What is involved in teamwork? The component parts are:
1. Members
2. A leader
3. Goals
4. Plans
5. Cooperation
6. Spirit

E. Principles of Organization
1. A team member must know what his job is.
2. Be sure that the nature and scope of a job are understood.
3. Authority and responsibility should be carefully spelled out.
4. A supervisor should be permitted to make the maximum number of decisions affecting his employees.
5. Employees should report to only one supervisor.
6. A supervisor should direct only as many employees as he can handle effectively.
7. An organization plan should be flexible.

8. Inspection and performance of work should be separate.
9. Organizational problems should receive immediate attention.
10. Assign work in line with ability and experience.

F. The Four Important Parts of Every Job
1. Inherent in every job is the *accountability* for results.
2. A second set of factors in every job is *responsibilities*.
3. Along with duties and responsibilities one must have the *authority* to act within certain limits without obtaining permission to proceed.
4. No job exists in a vacuum. The supervisor is surrounded by key *relationships*.

G. Principles of Delegation
Where work is delegated for the first time, the supervisor should think in terms of these questions:
1. Who is best qualified to do this?
2. Can an employee improve his abilities by doing this?
3. How long should an employee spend on this?
4. Are there any special problems for which he will need guidance?
5. How broad a delegation can I make?

H. Principles of Effective Communications
1. Determine the media.
2. To whom directed?
3. Identification and source authority.
4. Is communication understood?

I. Principles of Work Improvement
1. Most people usually do only the work which is assigned to them.
2. Workers are likely to fit assigned work into the time available to perform it.
3. A good workload usually stimulates output.
4. People usually do their best work when they know that results will be reviewed or inspected.
5. Employees usually feel that someone else is responsible for conditions of work, workplace layout, job methods, type of tools/equipment, and other such factors.
6. Employees are usually defensive about their job security.
7. Employees have natural resistance to change.
8. Employees can support or destroy a supervisor.
9. A supervisor usually earns the respect of his people through his personal example of diligence and efficiency.

J. Areas of Job Improvement
The areas of job improvement are quite numerous, but the most common ones which a supervisor can identify and utilize are:
1. Departmental layout
2. Flow of work
3. Workplace layout
4. Utilization of manpower
5. Work methods
6. Materials handling

7. Utilization
8. Motion economy

K. Seven Key Points in Making Improvements
1. Select the job to be improved
2. Study how it is being done now
3. Question the present method
4. Determine actions to be taken
5. Chart proposed method
6. Get approval and apply
7. Solicit worker participation

L. Corrective Techniques of Job Improvement
Specific Problems
1. Size of workload
2. Inability to meet schedules
3. Strain and fatigue
4. Improper use of men and skills
5. Waste, poor quality, unsafe conditions
6. Bottleneck conditions that hinder output
7. Poor utilization of equipment and machine
8. Efficiency and productivity of labor

General Improvement
1. Departmental layout
2. Flow of work
3. Work plan layout
4. Utilization of manpower
5. Work methods
6. Materials handling
7. Utilization of equipment
8. Motion economy

Corrective Techniques
1. Study with scale model
2. Flow chart study
3. Motion analysis
4. Comparison of units produced to standard allowance
5. Methods analysis
6. Flow chart and equipment study
7. Down time vs. running time
8. Motion analysis

M. A Planning Checklist
1. Objectives
2. Controls
3. Delegations
4. Communications
5. Resources
6. Manpower

7. Equipment
8. Supplies and materials
9. Utilization of time
10. Safety
11. Money
12. Work
13. Timing of improvements

N. Five Characteristics of Good Directions
In order to get results, directions must be:
1. Possible of accomplishment
2. Agreeable with worker interests
3. Related to mission
4. Planned and complete
5. Unmistakably clear

O. Types of Directions
1. Demands or direct orders
2. Requests
3. Suggestion or implication
4. volunteering

P. Controls
A typical listing of the overall areas in which the supervisor should establish controls might be:
1. Manpower
2. Materials
3. Quality of work
4. Quantity of work
5. Time
6. Space
7. Money
8. Methods

Q. Orienting the New Employee
1. Prepare for him
2. Welcome the new employee
3. Orientation for the job
4. Follow-up

R. Checklist for Orienting New Employees   Yes   No
1. Do you appreciate the feelings of new employees
   when they first report for work?   ___   ___
2. Are you aware of the fact that the new employee must
   make a big adjustment to his job?   ___   ___
3. Have you given him good reasons for liking the job and
   the organization?   ___   ___
4. Have you prepared for his first day on the job?   ___   ___
5. Did you welcome him cordially and make him feel needed?   ___   ___

		Yes	No

6. Did you establish rapport with him so that he feels free to talk and discuss matters with you? ___ ___
7. Did you explain his job to him and his relationship to you? ___ ___
8. Does he know that his work will be evaluated periodically on a basis that is fair and objective? ___ ___
9. Did you introduce him to his fellow workers in such a way that they are likely to accept him? ___ ___
10. Does he know what employee benefits he will receive? ___ ___
11. Does he understand the importance of being on the job and what to do if he must leave his duty station? ___ ___
12. Has he been impressed with the importance of accident prevention and safe practice? ___ ___
13. Does he generally know his way around the department? ___ ___
14. Is he under the guidance of a sponsor who will teach the right way of doing things? ___ ___
15. Do you plan to follow-up so that he will continue to adjust successfully to his job? ___ ___

S. Principles of Learning
1. Motivation
2. Demonstration or explanation
3. Practice

T. Causes of Poor Performance
1. Improper training for job
2. Wrong tools
3. Inadequate directions
4. Lack of supervisory follow-up
5. Poor communications
6. Lack of standards of performance
7. Wrong work habits
8. Low morale
9. Other

U. Four Major Steps in On-The-Job Instruction
1. Prepare the worker
2. Present the operation
3. Tryout performance
4. Follow-up

V. Employees Want Five Things
1. Security
2. Opportunity
3. Recognition
4. Inclusion
5. Expression

W. Some Don'ts in Regard to Praise
   1. Don't praise a person for something he hasn't done.
   2. Don't praise a person unless you can be sincere.
   3. Don't be sparing in praise just because your superior withholds it from you.
   4. Don't let too much time elapse between good performance and recognition of it

X. How to Gain Your Workers' Confidence
   Methods of developing confidence include such things as:
   1. Knowing the interests, habits, hobbies of employees
   2. Admitting your own inadequacies
   3. Sharing and telling of confidence in others
   4. Supporting people when they are in trouble
   5. Delegating matters that can be well handled
   6. Being frank and straightforward about problems and working conditions
   7. Encouraging others to bring their problems to you
   8. Taking action on problems which impede worker progress

Y. Sources of Employee Problems
   On-the-job causes might be such things as:
   1. A feeling that favoritism is exercised in assignments
   2. Assignment of overtime
   3. An undue amount of supervision
   4. Changing methods or systems
   5. Stealing of ideas or trade secrets
   6. Lack of interest in job
   7. Threat of reduction in force
   8. Ignorance or lack of communications
   9. Poor equipment
   10. Lack of knowing how supervisor feels toward employee
   11. Shift assignments

   Off-the-job problems might have to do with:
   1. Health
   2. Finances
   3. Housing
   4. Family

Z. The Supervisor's Key to Discipline
   There are several key points about discipline which the supervisor should keep in mind:
   1. Job discipline is one of the disciplines of life and is directed by the supervisor.
   2. It is more important to correct an employee fault than to fix blame for it.
   3. Employee performance is affected by problems both on the job and off.
   4. Sudden or abrupt changes in behavior can be indications of important employee problems.
   5. Problems should be dealt with as soon as possible after they are identified.
   6. The attitude of the supervisor may have more to do with solving problems than the techniques of problem solving.
   7. Correction of employee behavior should be resorted to only after the supervisor is sure that training or counseling will not be helpful.

8. Be sure to document your disciplinary actions.
9. Make sure that you are disciplining on the basis of facts rather than personal feelings.
10. Take each disciplinary step in order, being careful not to make snap judgments, or decisions based on impatience.

AA. Five Important Processes of Management
1. Planning
2. Organizing
3. Scheduling
4. Controlling
5. Motivating

BB. When the Supervisor Fails to Plan
1. Supervisor creates impression of not knowing his job
2. May lead to excessive overtime
3. Job runs itself—supervisor lacks control
4. Deadlines and appointments missed
5. Parts of the work go undone
6. Work interrupted by emergencies
7. Sets a bad example
8. Uneven workload creates peaks and valleys
9. Too much time on minor details at expense of more important tasks

CC. Fourteen General Principles of Management
1. Division of work
2. Authority and responsibility
3. Discipline
4. Unity of command
5. Unity of direction
6. Subordination of individual interest to general interest
7. Remuneration of personnel
8. Centralization
9. Scalar chain
10. Order
11. Equity
12. Stability of tenure of personnel
13. Initiative
14. Esprit de corps

DD. Change

Bringing about change is perhaps attempted more often, and yet less well understood, than anything else the supervisor does. How do people generally react to change? (People tend to resist change that is imposed upon them by other individuals or circumstances.

Change is characteristic of every situation. It is a part of every real endeavor where the efforts of people are concerned.

1. Why do people resist change?
   People may resist change because of:
   a. Fear of the unknown
   b. Implied criticism
   c. Unpleasant experiences in the past
   d. Fear of loss of status
   e. Threat to the ego
   f. Fear of loss of economic stability

2. How can we best overcome the resistance to change?
   In initiating change, take these steps:
   a. Get ready to sell
   b. Identify sources of help
   c. Anticipate objections
   d. Sell benefits
   e. Listen in depth
   f. Follow up

II. Brief Topical Summaries

   A. Who/What is the Supervisor?
      1. The supervisor is often called the "highest level employee and the lowest level manager."
      2. A supervisor is a member of both management and the work group. He acts as a bridge between the two.
      3. Most problems in supervision are in the area of human relations, or people problems.
      4. Employees expect: Respect, opportunity to learn and to advance, and a sense of belonging, and so forth.
      5. Supervisors are responsible for directing people and organizing work. Planning is of paramount importance.
      6. A position description is a set of duties and responsibilities inherent to a given position.
      7. It is important to keep the position description up-to-date and to provide each employee with his own copy.

   B. The Sociology of Work
      1. People are alike in many ways; however, each individual is unique.
      2. The supervisor is challenged in getting to know employee differences. Acquiring skills in evaluating individuals is an asset.
      3. Maintaining meaningful working relationships in the organization is of great importance.
      4. The supervisor has an obligation to help individuals to develop to their fullest potential.
      5. Job rotation on a planned basis helps to build versatility and to maintain interest and enthusiasm in work groups.
      6. Cross training (job rotation) provides backup skills.

7. The supervisor can help reduce tension by maintaining a sense of humor, providing guidance to employees, and by making reasonable and timely decisions. Employees respond favorably to working under reasonably predictable circumstances.
8. Change is characteristic of all managerial behavior. The supervisor must adjust to changes in procedures, new methods, technological changes, and to a number of new and sometimes challenging situations.
9. To overcome the natural tendency for people to resist change, the supervisor should become more skillful in initiating change.

C. Principles and Practices of Supervision
1. Employees should be required to answer to only one superior.
2. A supervisor can effectively direct only a limited number of employees, depending upon the complexity, variety, and proximity of the jobs involved.
3. The organizational chart presents the organization in graphic form. It reflects lines of authority and responsibility as well as interrelationships of units within the organization.
4. Distribution of work can be improved through an analysis using the "Work Distribution Chart."
5. The "Work Distribution Chart" reflects the division of work within a unit in understandable form.
6. When related tasks are given to an employee, he has a better chance of increasing his skills through training.
7. The individual who is given the responsibility for tasks must also be given the appropriate authority to insure adequate results.
8. The supervisor should delegate repetitive, routine work. Preparation of recurring reports, maintaining leave and attendance records are some examples.
9. Good discipline is essential to good task performance. Discipline is reflected in the actions of employees on the job in the absence of supervision.
10. Disciplinary action may have to be taken when the positive aspects of discipline have failed. Reprimand, warning, and suspension are examples of disciplinary action.
11. If a situation calls for a reprimand, be sure it is deserved and remember it is to be done in private.

D. Dynamic Leadership
1. A style is a personal method or manner of exerting influence.
2. Authoritarian leaders often see themselves as the source of power and authority.
3. The democratic leader often perceives the group as the source of authority and power.
4. Supervisors tend to do better when using the pattern of leadership that is most natural for them.
5. Social scientists suggest that the effective supervisor use the leadership style that best fits the problem or circumstances involved.
6. All four styles—telling, selling, consulting, joining—have their place. Using one does not preclude using the other at another time.

7. The theory X point of view assumes that the average person dislikes work, will avoid it whenever possible, and must be coerced to achieve organizational objectives.
8. The theory Y point of view assumes that the average person considers work to be a natural as play, and, when the individual is committed, he requires little supervision or direction to accomplish desired objectives.
9. The leader's basic assumptions concerning human behavior and human nature affect his actions, decisions, and other managerial practices.
10. Dissatisfaction among employees is often present, but difficult to isolate. The supervisor should seek to weaken dissatisfaction by keeping promises, being sincere and considerate, keeping employees informed, and so forth.
11. Constructive suggestions should be encouraged during the natural progress of the work.

E. Processes for Solving Problems
1. People find their daily tasks more meaningful and satisfying when they can improve them.
2. The causes of problems, or the key factors, are often hidden in the background. Ability to solve problems often involves the ability to isolate them from their backgrounds. There is some substance to the cliché that some persons "can't see the forest for the trees."
3. New procedures are often developed from old ones. Problems should be broken down into manageable parts. New ideas can be adapted from old one.
4. People think differently in problem-solving situations. Using a logical, patterned approach is often useful. One approach found to be useful includes these steps:
   a. Define the problem
   b. Establish objectives
   c. Get the facts
   d. Weigh and decide
   e. Take action
   f. Evaluate action

F. Training for Results
1. Participants respond best when they feel training is important to them.
2. The supervisor has responsibility for the training and development of those who report to him.
3. When training is delegated to others, great care must be exercised to insure the trainer has knowledge, aptitude, and interest for his work as a trainer.
4. Training (learning) of some type goes on continually. The most successful supervisor makes certain the learning contributes in a productive manner to operational goals.
5. New employees are particularly susceptible to training. Older employees facing new job situations require specific training, as well as having need for development and growth opportunities.
6. Training needs require continuous monitoring.
7. The training officer of an agency is a professional with a responsibility to assist supervisors in solving training problems.

8. Many of the self-development steps important to the supervisor's own growth are equally important to the development of peers and subordinates. Knowledge of these is important when the supervisor consults with others on development and growth opportunities.

G. Health, Safety, and Accident Prevention
1. Management-minded supervisors take appropriate measures to assist employees in maintaining health and in assuring safe practices in the work environment.
2. Effective safety training and practices help to avoid injury and accidents.
3. Safety should be a management goal. All infractions of safety which are observed should be corrected without exception.
4. Employees' safety attitude, training and instruction, provision of safe tools and equipment, supervision, and leadership are considered highly important factors which contribute to safety and which can be influenced directly by supervisors.
5. When accidents do occur, they should be investigated promptly for very important reasons, including the fact that information which is gained can be used to prevent accidents in the future.

H. Equal Employment Opportunity
1. The supervisor should endeavor to treat all employees fairly, without regard to religion, race, sex, or national origin.
2. Groups tend to reflect the attitude of the leader. Prejudice can be detected even in very subtle form. Supervisors must strive to create a feeling of mutual respect and confidence in every employee.
3. Complete utilization of all human resources is a national goal. Equitable consideration should be accorded women in the work force, minority-group members, the physically and mentally handicapped, and the older employee. The important question is: "Who can do the job?"
4. Training opportunities, recognition for performance, overtime assignments, promotional opportunities, and all other personnel actions are to be handled on an equitable basis.

I. Improving Communications
1. Communications is achieving understanding between the sender and the receiver of a message. It also means sharing information—the creation of understanding.
2. Communication is basic to all human activity. Words are means of conveying meanings; however, real meanings are in people.
3. There are very practical differences in the effectiveness of one-way, impersonal, and two-way communications. Words spoken face-to-face are better understood. Telephone conversations are effective, but lack the rapport of person-to-person exchanges. The whole person communicates.
4. Cooperation and communication in an organization go hand in hand. When there is a mutual respect between people, spelling out rules and procedures for communicating is unnecessary.
5. There are several barriers to effective communications. These include failure to listen with respect and understanding, lack of skill in feedback, and misinterpreting the meanings of words used by the speaker. It is also common

practice to listen to what we want to hear, and tune out things we do not want to hear.
6. Communication is management's chief problem. The supervisor should accept the challenge to communicate more effectively and to improve interagency and intra-agency communications.
7. The supervisor may often plan for and conduct meetings. The planning phase is critical and may determine the success or the failure of a meeting.
8. Speaking before groups usually requires extra effort. Stage fright may never disappear completely, but it can be controlled.

J. Self-Development
1. Every employee is responsible for his own self-development.
2. Toastmaster and toastmistress clubs offer opportunities to improve skills in oral communications.
3. Planning for one's own self-development is of vital importance. Supervisors know their own strengths and limitations better than anyone else.
4. Many opportunities are open to aid the supervisor in his developmental efforts, including job assignments; training opportunities, both governmental and non-governmental—to include universities and professional conferences and seminars.
5. Programmed instruction offers a means of studying at one's own rate.
6. Where difficulties may arise from a supervisor's being away from his work for training, he may participate in televised home study or correspondence courses to meet his self-development needs.

K. Teaching and Training
1. The Teaching Process
Teaching is encouraging and guiding the learning activities of students toward established goals. In most cases this process consists of five steps: preparation, presentation, summarization, evaluation, and application.

   a. Preparation
   Preparation is two-fold in nature; that of the supervisor and the employee. Preparation by the supervisor is absolutely essential to success. He must know what, when, where, how, and whom he will teach. Some of the factors that should be considered are:
   1) The objectives
   2) The materials needed
   3) The methods to be used
   4) Employee participation
   5) Employee interest
   6) Training aids
   7) Evaluation
   8) Summarization

   Employee preparation consists in preparing the employee to receive the material. Probably the most important single factor in the preparation of the employee is arousing and maintaining his interest. He must know the objectives of the training, why he is there, how the material can be used, and its importance to him.

b. Presentation
In presentation, have a carefully designed plan and follow it. The plan should be accurate and complete, yet flexible enough to meet situations as they arise. The method of presentation will be determined by the particular situation and objectives.

c. Summary
A summary should be made at the end of every training unit and program. In addition, there may be internal summaries depending on the nature of the material being taught. The important thing is that the trainee must always be able to understand how each part of the new material relates to the whole.

d. Application
The supervisor must arrange work so the employee will be given a chance to apply new knowledge or skills while the material is still clear in his mind and interest is high. The trainee does not really know whether he has learned the material until he has been given a chance to apply it. If the material is not applied, it loses most of its value.

e. Evaluation
The purpose of all training is to promote learning. To determine whether the training has been a success or failure, the supervisor must evaluate this learning.
In the broadest sense, evaluation includes all the devices, methods, skills, and techniques used by the supervisor to keep himself and the employees informed as to their progress toward the objectives they are pursuing. The extent to which the employee has mastered the knowledge, skills, and abilities, or changed his attitudes, as determined by the program objectives, is the extent to which instruction has succeeded or failed.
Evaluation should not be confined to the end of the lesson, day, or program but should be used continuously. We shall note later the way this relates to the rest of the teaching process.

2. Teaching Methods
A teaching method is a pattern of identifiable student and instructor activity used in presenting training material.
All supervisors are faced with the problem of deciding which method should be used at a given time.

a. Lecture
The lecture is direct oral presentation of material by the supervisor. The present trend is to place less emphasis on the trainer's activity and more on that of the trainee.

b. Discussion
Teaching by discussion or conference involves using questions and other techniques to arouse interest and focus attention upon certain areas, and by doing so creating a learning situation. This can be one of the most

valuable methods because it gives the employees an opportunity to express their ideas and pool their knowledge.

c. Demonstration
The demonstration is used to teach how something works or how to do something. It can be used to show a principle or what the results of a series of actions will be. A well-staged demonstration is particularly effective because it shows proper methods of performance in a realistic manner.

d. Performance
Performance is one of the most fundamental of all learning techniques or teaching methods. The trainee may be able to tell how a specific operation should be performed but he cannot be sure he knows how to perform the operation until he has done so.
As with all methods, there are certain advantages and disadvantages to each method.

e. Which Method to Use
Moreover, there are other methods and techniques of teaching. It is difficult to use any method without other methods entering into it. In any learning situation, a combination of methods is usually more effective than any one method alone.

Finally, evaluation must be integrated into the other aspects of the teaching-learning process.

It must be used in the motivation of the trainees; it must be used to assist in developing understanding during the training; and it must be related to employee application of the results of training.

This is distinctly the role of the supervisor.

BASIC FUNDAMENTALS OF STATISTICS

TABLE OF CONTENTS

		Page
I.	SCORES: THEIR MEANINGS AND FORMS	1
	a. Discrete and Continuous Scores	1
	b. Raw and Derived Scores	1
II.	THE ARRANGEMENT	1
	a. Rank Order	1
	b. Tabulation	2
	c. Graphical Representation	2
III.	MEASURES OF CENTRAL TENDENCY, OR AVERAGES	2
	a. The Median (Mdn.)	2
	b. The Mean (M)	3
	c. The Mode	3
IV.	MEASURES OF THE DISTRIBUTION OF SCORES	3
	a. The Normal Curve	3
	b. Importance of Measures of Distribution	3
	c. Measures of Distribution	4
	i. The Range	4
	ii. The Average Deviation (A.D.)	4
	iii. The Standard Deviation (S.D.)	4
	iv. The Probable Error (P.E.)	5
	v. The Quartile Deviation (Q)	5
V.	DERIVED SCORES	5
	a. Percent Scores	5
	b. Distance from the Average	5
	c. Percentile Scores	5
	d. T Scores	6
	e. Mental Age (M.A.)	6
	f. Intelligence Quotient (I.Q.)	6
	g. Educational Age	7
	h. Educational Quotient (E.Q.)	7
	i. Achievement Quotient (A.Q.)	7
	j. Norms	7
VI.	COMPARISONS OF GROUPS	7
VII.	CORRELATION	7
	a. Interpretation of the Coefficient of Correlation	8
	b. Uses of Correlation	8
	c. Reliability	8
	d. Validity	9
APPENDIX		10
	Table 1 – Calculation of the Mean, Median and Q	10
	Table 2 – Calculation of the A.D., S.D., and P.E.	12
	Table 3 – Calculation of the Rank-Difference Coefficient of Correlation	12

Basic Fundamentals of Statistics

I. SCORES: THEIR MEANINGS AND FORMS

"Whatever exists, exists in some amount."

As soon as measurements of any sort advance beyond the primitive statement that one thing is greater than, equal to, or less than another thing, we find the attempt to state results in numerical terms.

The meaning of such numerical statements should be clearly understood.

  A. Discrete and Continuous Scores

  There are certain kinds of measurement that result in scores that are *discrete* in the sense that there exist real gaps between the possible measurements that one can obtain. Thus the number of children in a family, or bills in a purse, increases only by whole numbers; one cannot find 5 1/2 children, or 7 1/4 bills, unless one practices mutilation. Other measures give *continuous* scores in the sense that the scores are theoretically capable of any degree of subdivision. Scores on tests are usually given in units, as 68 or 75; but with more accurate tests, scores of 77.4 or 86.273 would also be possible. Nearly all measurements in psychology and education deal with continuous series of scores rather than with discrete series, and the following discussion deals throughout with the statistical treatment of continuous series. Some modification of the formulas used with continuous series is necessary before one can apply them to discrete series.

  B. Raw and Derived Scores

  The score actually obtained in making a measurement is called a *raw score*. If a pupil makes a score of 59 on a test, that is his raw score. Raw scores do not by themselves indicate if they are high or low; a score of 59 might be high on one test and low on another. If a pupil made a score of 59 on an intelligence test, that might be translated to mean that he achieved a mental age of 12 years, an IQ of 108, a percentile rank of 78, etc. All these interpretative measures would be called *derived scores,* as they are derived from the raw score. A derived score tells us much more about the quality of a performance than the raw score does. Many kinds of derived scores will be described below.

II. THE ARRANGEMENT

Suppose that a certain class takes a test and makes the following scores: 92, 88, 97, 95, 100, 58, 90, 94, 72, 91, 83, 88, 83, 87, 82, 78, 64, 69, 97, 95, 86, 85, 85, 89, 77, 61, 74, 59. Until we arrange them in some different way we cannot tell much about these scores. (Note: most of the computations in the Appendix are based on this series of scores.)

  A. Rank Order

  With a small number of scores, it is often profitable to arrange them in rank order, with the highest at one end and the lowest at the other. From the rank order one can very easily determine the highest score, the lowest score, the midscore and percentile scores. One method of correlation is based on the rank order. Confusion will be avoided if the lowest score is always given rank one. The only difficulty that arises in constructing a rank order is in regard to tie scores. In such a case, the ranks covered by the tied scores are averaged, and that average rank is given to each. Example: If two scores are tied for second rank, they cover ranks two and three; $\frac{2+3}{5} = 2.5$, and than rank is given to each. The next following score is given rank four. If the ranking is done properly, the last score should come out with a rank equal to the number of scores, except where there is a tie for last place.

B. Tabulation

Tabulation consists essentially in dividing the scores into groups, all groups covering equal portions of the total range of scores, and arranging the groups in rank order. When the groups, which are called *classes,* are arranged in a vertical column, and the number of scores falling in each class is indicated by a number, the tabulation is called a *frequency distribution.* A frequency distribution gives us a fairly clear picture of the way the scores are distributed. It is necessary to get the frequency distribution before one can represent the results graphically, or use any of the shortcut methods of computation. It usually takes less time to tabulate scores than it does to rank them, unless the number of scores is very small.

Before tabulating, it is necessary to choose the size of the class interval to be used. To do this, first subtract the lowest from the highest score, getting the range. Choose as the size of the interval a number that will divide the range into not less than 10 or more than 20 classes. Arrange the classes in a vertical column, with the highest at the top. In table 1, Appendix, a class interval of 5 has been used. Note that the lowest class, 55-59.99, means anything from 55.0 up to but not including 60; and that its midpoint is 57.5, not 57.0. Often the class is written simply as 55-59; in that case, it really means 55.0-59.99. For each score in the series, place a tally (/) to the right of the class in which the score belongs. The frequency column simply states in numbers the number of tallies, or scores, in each class.

C. Graphical Representation

A graph, or pictorial representation, often tells a story much more vividly than a table. There are two main kinds of graphs for representing score distributions, the histogram and the frequency polygon. In both, the classes are represented by equal distances along a horizontal line, with the lowest at the left. The difference is that in the histogram a horizontal line is drawn above the class to indicate the number of scores, and these lines are connected by vertical lines; while in the frequency polygon the number of scores is represented by a dot above the midpoint of the class, and the dots are joined by straight lines. Note that the histogram represents each score by a similar unit of area; the frequency polygon does not. The frequency polygon is generally used when two or more distributions are to be compared graphically, as similarities and differences in shape stand out more clearly, due to the oblique lines, than they do with histograms. The Appendix contains a histogram and a frequency polygon for the same set of scores.

III. MEASURES OF CENTRAL TENDENCY, OR AVERAGES

There are several kinds of averages, or measures of central tendency, of which only three -- the median, the mean, and the mode -- are used to any extent in psychological and educational measurement. All averages represent the whole distribution of scores by a single number. It must be remembered that most score distributions contain some scores that are far from the average. Nevertheless, the average is the most useful single statistical measure that one can find out about a group of scores.

A. The Median (Mdn.)

The median is that value such that half of the scores are greater than or equal to it, and half of the scores are less than or equal to it. If the scores are arranged in rank order, the median is the middle score, or mid-score, and can be obtained by counting from either end of the rank order. Note that the extreme scores can be either close to or far from the median without affecting its computation.

The median is preferable to the mean when quick computation is desired; when extreme or inaccurate scores should not influence the average; and when percentile scores are to be obtained. The norms (see below for the meaning of this term) of many intelligence and educational tests are stated in terms of median and percentile scores, and when using such tests the median is to be preferred to the mean.

B. The Mean (M)

The mean is the measure popularly called "the average" and can be simply obtained by adding together all of the scores and dividing by the number

$M = \frac{\Sigma m}{N}$ In the Formula means "sum of," m refers to an individual score, and N

means the number of scores. The exact size of each score counts in finding the mean, while only the scores near the middle of the distribution are important in determining the median. The mean should be used when a standard deviation or coefficient of correlation is to be found, and when every score should count in the average. It involves somewhat more arithmetical computation than the median.

Unless the number of cases is small, time can be saved by computing the mean from scores grouped in a frequency distribution, rather than from ungrouped scores. Multiply the midpoint of each class by the frequency in that class; i.e.,

$M = \frac{F \times Midpoint}{N}$. A still shorter method is available, in which one takes the mid-

point of some class as a guessed mean, and then calculates a correction which is added to the guessed mean. This is profitable when the number of scores is fairly large. For details of this "short method," consult a standard text.

C. The Mode

The mode is simply the score that occurs the greatest number of times. There may be more than one mode in a score distribution. When the scores are grouped, the midpoint of the class that contains the greatest frequency is called the crude mode. The mode is greatly influenced by chance factors, and so is ordinarily of not much significance. It should be used when one wants the most frequent score, or when one wants a very rough average without calculation.

IV. MEASURES OF THE DISTRIBUTION OF SCORES

A. The Normal Curve

Scores in a great many human traits distribute themselves so as to form a symmetrical, bell-shaped frequency polygon, which is called a normal curve, normal distribution curve, normal probability curve, etc. Normal curves are obtained when the results are influenced by a large number of factors, each acting separately in an apparently chance way. For instance, if one tosses 20 pennies 1000 times, and plots the number of times each possible combination of heads and tails comes out, the results will form a normal curve. The normal curve is very important statistically, because all normal curves have similar statistical properties. Knowing the mean and standard deviation of a normal curve, one can deduce all of the other characteristics of the distribution. In a perfectly normal curve the mean, median, and mode all fall on the same score. Very often distributions are obtained which closely approximate normal distributions, but are not exactly normal; if the difference is slight, they may be treated as normal curves. When a distribution is lop-sided, with the scores piled up more on one side of the mean than on the other, it is said to be skewed. A large departure from the true normal curve may be due to a small number of cases, or may indicate that the trait is distributed in a way that is not fundamentally normal.

B. Importance of Measures of Distribution

Two groups may have the same average scores on a test, but be widely different. All the members of one class may make very similar scores, while the members of the other class may differ widely. For instance, 3, 6, 9, 12, and 15 have the same mean as 7, 8, 9, 10, and 11. This matter of the spread, scattering, variability, or distribution of scores is often very important. It can be roughly estimated from a graph, but for accuracy one of several available statistical measures should be used. These measures of distribution are really valid only for distributions that are fundamentally normal.

C. Measures of Distribution
1. The Range is simply the difference between the highest and lowest scores. It is the easiest measure of distribution to obtain, but the least dependable, because factors that have little effect on the distribution as a whole may have a marked effect on the on the extreme scores.
2. The Average Deviation (A.D.), sometimes called the mean deviation, is the mean of the deviations of the separate scores from the mean. The deviation of any score is the difference between that score and the mean. In getting the mean of the deviations, no attention is paid to plus and minus signs. Although relatively easy to obtain, the A.D. is less useful than the standard deviation, and. is being used less and less.

With grouped scores, the A.D. can be obtained by getting the deviation of each class midpoint from the mean. Each deviation is then multipled by the corresponding frequency. The mean of these deviations is then obtained, disregarding plus and minus signs. A "short method," in which deviations are taken from a guessed mean and a correction applied afterward, saves arithmetic because it eliminates multiplying by numbers containing decimals.

3. The Standard Deviation (S.D. or the Greek letter sigma (6). In calculating this measure, the deviation of each score from the mean is obtained, as with the A.D. Instead of simply averaging the deviations, however, each deviation is squared before averaging, and the square root of the average is extracted. This square root is the standard deviation -- it is the square root of the mean of the squared deviations.

$$S.D. = \sqrt{\frac{\Sigma D^2}{N}}$$

The S.D. has many uses. It has a constant relationship to the shape of the normal curve. Knowing the mean and the S.D. of a normal distribution, one can determine the percent of the total number of scores that lie between any two scores, by referring to a special table. Approximately 68% of the scores in any normal curve lie between the mean and the scores 1 S.D. above and below the mean; approximately 95% lie between the mean and the scores 2 S.D.'s above and below the mean; and over 99% of the scores are less than 3 S.D.'s above or below the mean (see the illustration of a normal curve in the Appendix). If we wanted to compare the variability of one set of scores with that of another, we simply compare their S.D.'s; the one with the larger S.D. has the greater spread of scores. The S.D. is the most valuable of the various measures of distribution, although its computation takes longer than that of the A.D. or Q. It must be computed if one wants to get T Scores or a product-moment coefficient of correlation (These are explained below).

As with the M and A.D., arithmetic can be lessened by computing

$$S.D. = \frac{\Sigma (F D^2)}{N}$$

the S.D. from grouped scores. See Table 2 in the Appendix for examples of the calculation of the A.D. and S.D. from grouped scores. There is also a "short method" of computing the S.D., in which deviations are taken from a guessed mean, and a correction applied.

4. The Probable Error (P.E.). The P.E. is obtained by multiplying the S.D. by .6745. In a normal distribution exactly 50% of the cases lie between the mean and the scores one P.E. above or below the mean; the other 50% of the scores are more than one P.E. away from the mean. Practically all cases in a normal distribution are less than 4 P.E.'s away from the mean.

5. The Quartile Deviation (Q). One often wants to locate the middle 50% of a group of scores. The first quartile point, Q_1, is that score below or equal to which are 25%

of the scores in the distribution. The third quartile point, Q_3, is that score below or equal to which 75% of

the scores lie. The middle 50% of the scores can be found by subtracting Q_1 from Q_3

$$Q = \frac{Q_3 - Q_1}{2}$$

The quartile deviation is half of the range of scores. It is one-half of the range covered by the middle 50% of the scores. In a perfectly normal distribution Q and P.E. are identical. It is customary to use Q as the measure of variability when the median is used as the measure of central tendency.

V. DERIVED SCORES

If one is told that a person has made a score of 43 on a test, that in itself means very little, as the meaning of a score depends on many factors. The test itself may have a total possible score of 50, 100, or 150. The mean may be below 30 or above 70. The scores may be grouped closely together or spread over a wide range. For this reason a raw score must be interpreted in some way before it tells much about the goodness of the performance.

A. Percent Scores

Teachers often express scores in terms of the percent of the total possible score. An easy way to do this is to score the test so as to have a total possible score of 100. This is fairly satisfactory, but has some shortcomings. One teacher may give harder tests than another, or score of 85%. This sometimes happens when the students in the two classes have equal knowledge; sometimes the better class may get the lower average.

B. Distance from the Average

If we know that a score is 5 points above or below the mean or median, we know more about it than if we simply know the raw score or percent score. However, 5 points may be a big difference on one test and a small difference on another test.

C. Percentile Scores

A percentile score states the percent of the total number of scores that are below or equal to a particular score. For instance, the statement that the raw score of 67 on a test stands at the 83rd percentile means that 83% of the scores in the distribution are at or below 67. The median is the 50th percentile; Q_1 is the 25th percentile; Q_3 is the 75th percentile. The percentile score tells us not merely whether a score is above or below the median, but gives us also its exact place in the rank order. Because percentile scores are easy to compute and help greatly in the interpretation of scores, most psychological and educational tests designed for general use are accompanied by tables giving the percentile values of all of the possible raw scores on the test.

These values are based on results previously obtained with the test. Often separate percentile tables are given for each age or grade, so that one can determine just how each pupil in a group stands in comparison with the much larger group used in determining the tables.

Since in a normal distribution the scores are much more frequent near the median than they are near the extremes, percentile scores are not directly proportional in size to raw scores. For instance, there is more of a difference between the raw scores of two pupils with percentile ranks of 90 and 95 than there is between the ra.w scores of two pupils with percentile ranks of 50 and 55. For this reason one cannot combine a pupil's scores on different tests by averaging his percentile scores. The best way to average scores on different tests, with different averages and different variabilities, is to use T Scores, which are explained below.

To find the raw scores corresponding to any percentile value, first multiply N by the percentile value, and then count up that many scores from the bottom of the rank order, or down from the top. The median is the 50th percentile; to locate it, count 50% of the scores from either end of the rank order. The 60th percentile, in a group of 25 scores, is the 15th from the lowest. When the desired score is fractional, and when the percentile score is calculated from grouped scores, interpolation is necessary. In Table 1, Appendix, illustrations are given of the calculation of the Median, 25th percentile, 75th percentile, and Q. The calculation of the median may be explained as follows: 50% of N is 14. There are 12 scores below the 85 - 89.99 class, and 7 scores in that class; therefore the median is 2/7ths of the way up in that class. Since the class covers 5 scores, multiply 2/7ths by 5; add this to 85.0, the lower limit of the class, and the result is the median. Other percentiles are calculated in the same way.

D. T Scores

Since the S.D. has a constant relation to the shape of the normal curve, a score which is a certain distance above the mean on one test has the same relative value as a score which is the same distance above the mean on another test, if the distances are divided by the S.D. in each case, and equated on that basis. In other words, a score which is two S.D.'s above the mean on one test is equivalent to a score which is two S.D.'s above the mean on another test. T Scores are scores stated in terms of what fraction of an S.D. a score is above or below the mean. Because T Scores are always proportional to the raw scores, the T Scores of the same individual on different tests can be combined by simple averaging. This is the best way to combine scores from several different tests into a total score.

To translate raw scores into T Scores, first subtract the mean from each score, and divide each remainder by the S.D. This will be plus if the score is above the mean and minus if below the mean. Such scores are called "standard deviation scores." Multiply the standard deviation score by 10, and add 50; the result is a T Score. The possible range of T Scores is from 0 to 100, and the mean always has a T Score value of 50.

E. Mental Age (M.A.)

Mental age is a kind of derived score used with intelligence tests. The M.A. corresponding to any raw score may be defined as the age of the group of children who on the average make that raw score. Example: A child makes a score of 43 on an intelligence test. 43 is the average raw score on this test of children 9 years, 3 months old. The child's M.A. is therefore 9 years, 3 months. A child's mental age increases as he gets older. Children of different chronological ages (C.A.'s) may have the same M.A.'s.

F. Intelligence Quotient (I.Q.)

The I.Q. is the M.A. divided by the C.A. A child who is above average mentally always has an I.Q. above 100, and a child below average has an I.Q. below 100. The I.Q. remains roughly constant as a child grows older; it is an indication of the rate of mental growth, or brightness.

G. Educational Age (E.A.)

This is similar to the M.A., except that it applies only to tests of educational achievement or knowledge. A child has an E.A. of 10 years when he makes a score on an educational test equal to the average score of 10 year old children.

H. Educational Quotient (E.Q.)

This is the E.A. divided by the C.A. It indicates the rate of educational progress, while the E.A. indicates the present educational attainment. The E.A. and E.Q. are obtained from standardized tests covering several subjects. Ages and quotients can also be obtained for individual subjects, as reading age, reading quotient, arithmetic age, etc.

I. Achievement Quotient (A.Q.)

This is an indication of how a child's educational achievement compares with his intelligence. It is obtained by dividing the E.A. by the M.A., or by dividing the E.Q. by the I.Q. A child with an E.A. of 8 years an an M.A. of 10 years has an A.Q. of 80; a child with an E.Q. of 120 and an I.Q. of 100 has an A.Q. of 120.

J. Norms

Norms are groups of scores for a particular test which have been obtained from large groups of subjects, and which are used for interpreting new results obtained with the test. Percentile scores, T Scores, mental and educational ages and quotients are all different ways of stating the norms. Usually the author of an intelligence or achievement test states his norms in more than one of these ways. Another kind of norm sometimes used is the *grade norm,* where the average score given is for a grade rather than for a chronological age.

VI. COMPARISONS OF GROUPS

One often wants to compare the results of two groups on the same test. A simple statement of the means or medians of the two groups is not sufficient, because there may be much or little overlapping between the two groups (see examples at the right.) A commonly used device is to state the percent of one group that exceeds the median of the other group. If this is close to 50%, the amount of overlapping is great; if close to 0 or 100, the overlapping is relatively slight.

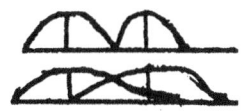

A problem that occurs frequently in psychological and educational measurement is the question whether a difference that has been found between two measures is reliable; in other words, would a similar difference be found again and again if the measurements were repeated. This is determined by comparing the obtained difference with the standard error of the difference, or the probable error of the difference. The exact meaning of these two statistical measures need not be explained here. Differences are not considered to be completely reliable unless they are at least three times their standard error or four times the probable error. Example: The mean I.Q. of another class; the standard error of the difference is 1.3 points. Since the difference is less than 3 times its standard error, it is not reliable -- it may be due purely to chance, and a repetition may show no such difference.

VII. CORRELATION

One often wants to know whether there is any relation between two sets of results obtained from the same subjects. The most frequently used method of measuring such a relationship is to calculate a coefficient of correlation. This is a quantitative measure of the degree of relationship between two sets of measures for the same group of individuals. There are two widely used methods of measuring correlation. The simpler of these is the rank-difference method, devised by Spearman. This is based on the comparison of the rank orders in the two sets of measures, disregarding the actual size of the raw scores. It is much easier to calculate, and is usually used when the number of cases is small. It is somewhat less accurate than the product-moment method, devised by Pearson, which uses the raw scores. The symbol for the coefficient of correlation obtained by the rank-difference method is the Greek letter rho; for the product-moment coefficient, the letter r.

The student who wishes to learn how to compute r should refer to a basic reference. The computation of rho is relatively simple, and will be briefly outlined. The rank order for each set of measures is first obtained. For each subject the two ranks are placed side by side. The D or difference column records the difference between the two ranks, for each subject. These differences are then squared, and the squared differences are added up. This total is multipled by 6, and is the numerator of a fraction. The denominator of the fraction is $N(N^2-1)$. Rho is obtained by subtracting the fraction from 1.00. Consult Table 3 for an illustration.

 A. Interpretation of the Coefficient of Correlation

  Coefficients of correlation range in size from plus 1.00 to minus 1.00. Both of these values indicate a perfect relationship or correspondence. Plus 1.00 indicates that the person with the highest score on one trait also has the highest score on the other, the second highest is also second highest on the second, etc. Minus 1.00 means that the highest on one trait is the lowest on the other, the second highest on one is next to the lowest on the other, etc. An r of zero indicates that there is a complete absence of relationship between the two sets of measurements; those high on one trait may be either high or low on the other. Intermediate values (+.53,-.40, etc.) are not percents, an an r of approximately .80 indicates only half as close a relationship an an r of 1.00. Customarily an r of less than .40 is considered low, .40 - .70 substantial, and above .70, high. But even an r of .80 contains an occasional marked exception to the general relationship. Before we can predict a person's score on one trait with accuracy from a knowledge of his score on another trait, we should have an r above .90 between the two traits.

  It should be noted that the presence of a correlation between two traits does not prove that one is the cause of the other; it merely indicates the presence of a relationship between the two. For instance, in an 8th grade class there is a minus correlation between height and I.Q. Neither of these traits is the cause of the other; the relationship is due to the fact that the younger children in the class are both smaller and brighter than the older children.

 B. Uses of Correlation

  One of the important uses of correlation is in *prediction*. If there is a high correlation between two traits, one can predict a person's score on one from a knowledge of his score on the other, with better than the chance success. A very high correlation, however, is necessary for accurate prediction.

 C. Reliability

  In using a test, it is important to know if the results obtained are close to what would be obtained if the measurements are repeated. By reliability we mean the extent to which the same test (or two equivalent forms of the same test) will give similar results when used on the same subjects more than once. Reliability is indicated by correlation. *Retest reliability* is the correlation between two sets of scores on the same test obtained from the same subjects. *Split-half reliability* is the correlation between scores on the two halves of a test; to make this comparable to retest reliability, a special formula (the Spearman-Brown Formula) is applied. A test to be really reliable, should have reliability over .90 as measured in both ways. Reliability is essentially the consistency with which a test will give the same results on repeated administration.

D. Validity

The validity of a test is its most important characteristic, and also the one hardest to measure. By validity we mean the degree of perfection to which a test measures what it is supposed to measure. Students often confuse validity with reliability. Remember that reliability measures the consistency of a test, the extent to which it will give the same results over and over again. A test may be reliable, without measuring what it is supposed to measure. For instance, one could measure the circumference of the skull very reliably, but the result would be an exceedingly poor indication of intelligence-- as a measure of intelligence this measure, although reliable, would be totally invalid. A history test consisting entirely of dates to be identified might give very reliable results, but they could be invalid as a measure of understanding the significance of historical events.

The usual way of measuring the validity of a test is to correlate the results with some criterion -- that is, with some other measure of the trait in question, which is already known to be valid. The big difficulty in establishing the validity of a new test is to find a satisfactory criterion. For instance, one should not look for an extremely high correlation with teacher's marks and estimates, because the test is expected to be a better measure than the teacher's marks are. Also, a perfect correlation with other tests that are known to be only partly valid is not desirable. Ordinarily a test is correlated with each of a few partly satisfactory criteria, and its validity is estimated from the results.

APPENDIX
Table 1 - Calculation of the Mean, Median, and Q

SCORES	MIDPOINT	TALLIES	F(FREQUENCY)	F x MIDPOINT
100-104.99	102.5	/	1	102.5
95- 99.99	97.5	////	4	390.0
90- 94.99	92.5	////	4	370.0
85- 89.99	87.5	++++ / /	7	612.5
80- 84.99	82.5	///	3	247.5
75- 79.99	77.5	//	2	155.0
70- 74.99	72.5	/	2	145.0
65- 69.99	67.5	//	1	67.5
60- 64.99	62.5	//	2	125.0
55- 59.99	57.5		2	115.0
			N = 28	2330.0

HISTORGRAM

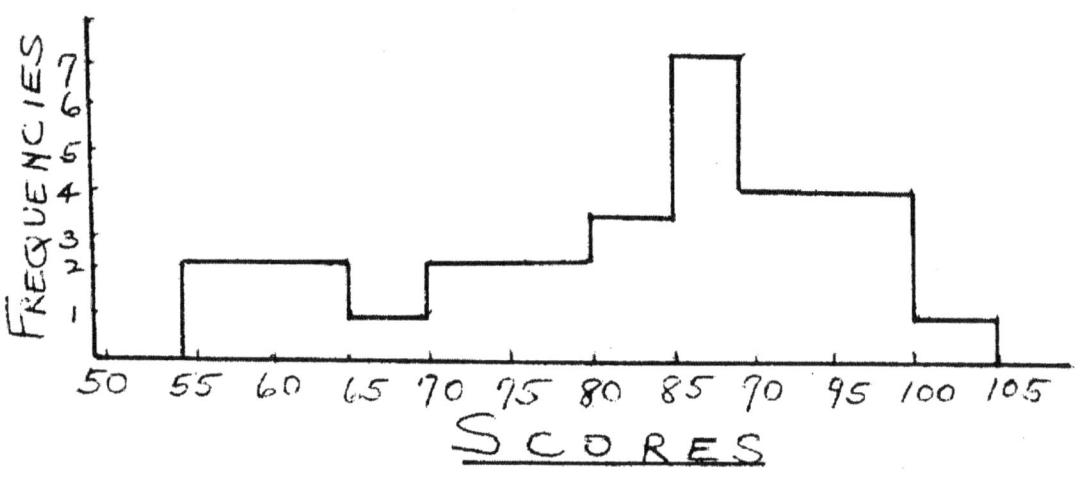

The Mean

$$M = \frac{(Fx\ Midpoint)}{N} = \frac{2330.0}{28} = 83.2$$

The Median

    50% of N = 14. There are 12 scores below the 85-89.99 interval, leaving 2 scores to go. There are 7 scores in that class, and the class covers 5 scores. 2/7 X 5 = 1.4.

    Median = 85.0 + 1.4 = 86.4

Frequency Polygon

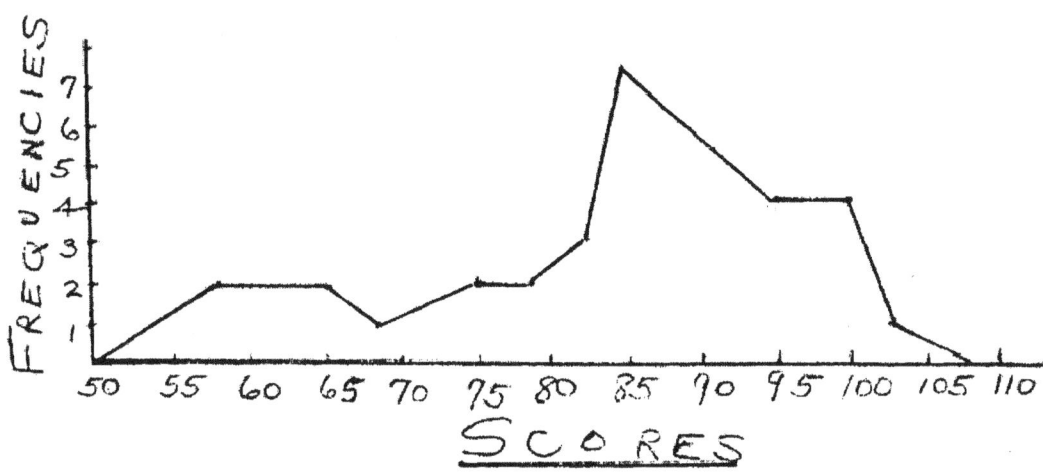

The Quartile Deviation

$$Q = \frac{Q_3 - Q_1}{2}$$

$$= \frac{92.5 - 75.0}{2}$$

$$= 8.75$$

$Q_3 =$ 75th percentile. 75% of 28 = 21. There are 19 scores below 90.0. 90.0 + 2/4 X 5 = 92.5

$Q_1 =$ 25th percentile. 25% of 28 = 7. 7 scores bring us exactly up to 75.0; therefore Q_1 = 75.0

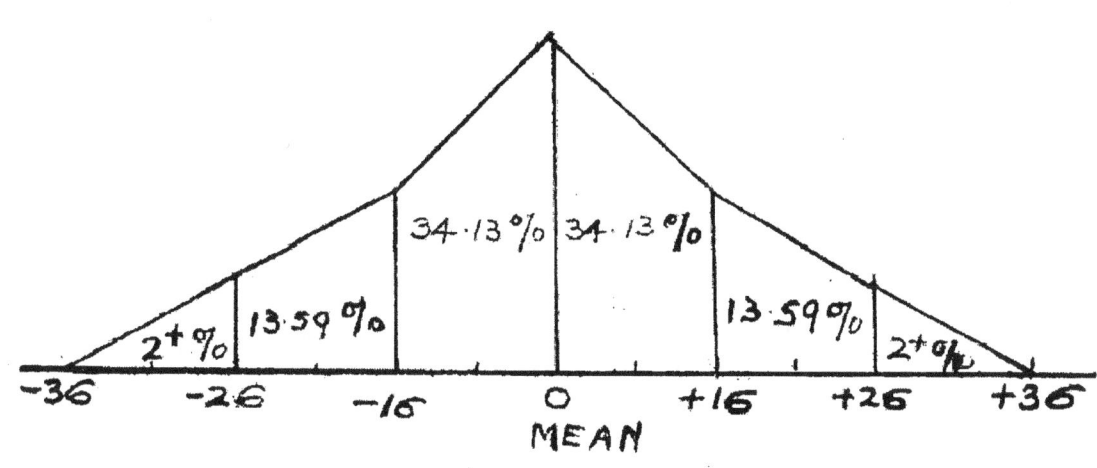

A THEORETICAL NORMAL CURVE

Table 2 - Calculation of the A. BY, S.D., and P.E.

SCORES	MIDPOINT	F	D(DEVIATION)	FD	FD²
100-104.99	102.5	1	19.3	19.3	372.49
95- 99.99	97.5	4	14.3	57.2	817.96
90- 94.99	92.5	4	9.3	37.2	345.96
85- 89.99	87.5	7	4.3	30.1	129.43
80- 84.99	82.5	3	- 0.7	- 2.1	1.47
75- 79.99	77.5	2	- 5.7	-11.4	64.98
70- 74.99	72.5	2	-10.7	-21.4	228.98
65- 69.99	67.5	1	-15.7	-15.7	246.49
60- 64.99	62.5	2	-20.7	-41.4	856.98
55- 59.99	57.5	2	-25.7	-51.4	1320.98
M= 83.2		N=28		257.2	4385.72

NOTES
1. For each class, the deviation is the difference between the mean and the midpoint of that class.
2. The FD² column is obtained by multiplying each FD by the corresponding D. It is F X D², not F² X D².
3. In adding up the FD column to get the A.D., the minus signs are disregarded. There are no minus signs in the FD²

The Average Deviation

$$A.D. = \frac{\Sigma FD}{N} = \frac{287.2}{28} = 10.29$$

The Standard Deviation

$$S.D. = \sqrt{\frac{\Sigma(FD^2)}{N}} = \sqrt{\frac{4385.72}{28}} = \sqrt{56.63} = 12.52$$

The Probable Error
P.E. = .6745 X S.D. = .6745 X 12.52 = 8.44

Table 3 - Calculation of the Rank-Difference Coefficient of Correlation

Individual	Score on Test 1	Score on Test 2	Rank on Test 1	Rank on Test 2	D	D
A	18	20	7	4	3	9
B	24	17	4	7	3	9
C	22	19	5	5.5	0.5	0.25
D	27	21	1.5	3	1.5	2.25
E	26	25	3	2	1	1
F	27	26	1.5	1	0.5	0.256
G	20	19	6	5.5	0.5	0.25
N = 7					ΣD²	=22.00

NOTES
1. Each entry in the "D" or difference column is the difference between the two ranks attained by that individual.
2. Note that, in getting the rank orders, two tied scores get the average of the two ranks covered; the following score gets the next rank.

$$\text{rho} = 1 - \frac{6 \Sigma D^2}{N(N^2 - 1)} = 1 - \frac{6 \times 22.00}{7(49-1)} = 1 - \frac{132}{336} = +.61$$